Business and Conflict in Fragile States:
the Case for Pragmatic Solutions

Brian Ganson and Achim Wennmann

Business and Conflict in Fragile States:
the Case for Pragmatic Solutions

Brian Ganson and Achim Wennmann

IISS The International Institute for Strategic Studies

The International Institute for Strategic Studies

Arundel House | 13–15 Arundel Street | Temple Place | London | WC2R 3DX | UK

First published June 2016 **Routledge**
4 Park Square, Milton Park, Abingdon, Oxon, OX14 4RN

for **The International Institute for Strategic Studies**
Arundel House, 13–15 Arundel Street, Temple Place, London, WC2R 3DX, UK
www.iiss.org

Simultaneously published in the USA and Canada by **Routledge**
270 Madison Ave., New York, NY 10016

Routledge is an imprint of Taylor & Francis, an Informa Business

© 2016 The International Institute for Strategic Studies

DIRECTOR-GENERAL AND CHIEF EXECUTIVE Dr John Chipman
EDITOR Dr Nicholas Redman
EDITORIAL Alice Aveson, Jill Lally, Nancy Turner
COVER/PRODUCTION John Buck
COVER IMAGE Community protest, May 2015, against the Tia Maria copper mining
project in Southern Peru; the sign translates as 'agriculture yes, mine no'. (Sebastian
Castañeda/Anadolu/Getty)

The International Institute for Strategic Studies is an independent centre for research,
information and debate on the problems of conflict, however caused, that have, or
potentially have, an important military content. The Council and Staff of the Institute
are international and its membership is drawn from almost 100 countries. The Institute
is independent and it alone decides what activities to conduct. It owes no allegiance to
any government, any group of governments or any political or other organisation. The
IISS stresses rigorous research with a forward-looking policy orientation and places
particular emphasis on bringing new perspectives to the strategic debate.

The Institute's publications are designed to meet the needs of a wider audience than its
own membership and are available on subscription, by mail order and in good book-
shops. Further details at www.iiss.org.

Printed and bound in Great Britain by Bell & Bain Ltd, Thornliebank, Glasgow

British Library Cataloguing in Publication Data
A catalogue record for this book is available from the British Library

Library of Congress Cataloging in Publication Data

ADELPHI series
ISSN 1944-5571

ADELPHI 457-458
ISBN 978-1-138-21397-5

Contents

ACKNOWLEDGEMENTS

The ideas presented in this book emerged as we worked, separately and together, on questions at the nexus of business and conflict in fragile states. Over many years of research and activity in the field, we have benefited from the critical reflections of our academic and practitioner colleagues on every continent in the business, development, security and peace-building communities. In an emerging area of enquiry for which the need for more systematic quantitative and qualitative analysis seems apparent, their insight has helped to calibrate the arguments presented, to ensure that necessarily broad generalities are grounded in real experience, and to maintain a focus on pragmatic and workable solutions. We wish to offer our sincere and heartfelt thanks to each of you. Any errors or omissions of fact or judgement are of course our own responsibility.

Brian Ganson and Achim Wennmann
Cape Town and Geneva, May 2016

GLOSSARY

ABN	ABN Amro
AfDB	African Development Bank
AMDC	African Minerals Development Centre
ANC	African National Congress (South Africa)
AU	African Union
AVRP	armed violence reduction and prevention
BIT	bilateral investment treaty
BSAC	British South Africa Company
CAO	Compliance Advisor Ombudsman (for IMF and MIGA)
CASA	Conflict Affected States in Africa (initiative of the IFC)
CBM	Consultative Business Movement (South Africa)
CBMS	community-based monitoring systems
CCMA	Commission for Conciliation, Mediation and Arbitration (South Africa)
CCSD	Center for Conflict, Security and Development (World Bank)
CKD	chronic kidney disease
CODESA	Convention for a Democratic South Africa
CoST	Construction Sector Transparency Initiative
CRMA	Crime and Risk Mapping Analysis (South Sudan)
DAC	Development Assistance Committee (OECD)
DRC	Democratic Republic of the Congo
EITI	Extractive Industries Transparency Initiative
FDI	foreign direct investment
FOE	Friends of the Earth
GAIN	Global Alliance for Improved Nutrition
GDP	gross domestic product

GDS	Geneva Declaration Secretariat
GIZ	German International Cooperation Agency
GMU	General Memorandum of Understanding
HRC	Human Rights Council (UN)
HRW	Human Rights Watch
IBRD	International Bank for Reconstruction and Development
ICJ	International Commission of Jurists
ICMM	International Council on Mining and Metals
ICRC	International Committee of the Red Cross
ICSID	International Centre for Settlement of Investment Disputes
IDA	International Development Association
IDP	internally displaced person
IDRC	International Development Research Centre
IEG	Independent Evaluation Group (World Bank)
IFC	International Finance Corporation
ILO	International Labour Organization
IMF	International Monetary Fund
IMSSA	Independent Mediation Service of South Africa
IRCA	International Railways of Central America
JICA	Japan International Cooperation Agency
LDCs	least developed countries
LICUS	low-income countries under stress (World Bank)
MARCO	Morris American Rubber Company
MIGA	Multilateral Investment Guarantee Agency
MILF	Moro Islamic Liberation Front (Philippines)
MNE	multinational enterprise
NDPI	Niger Delta Partnership Initiative
NGO	non-governmental organisation
NIC	National Intelligence Council (USA)
NRM	National Resistance Movement (Uganda)
OAS	Organization of American States
OCHA	United Nations Office for the Coordination of Humanitarian Affairs

OECD	Organisation for Economic Co-operation and Development
OEEC	Organisation for European Economic Co-operation
OHCHR	Office of the United Nations High Commissioner for Human Rights
P4P	Partners for Peace
PDIA	problem-driven iterative adaptation
PFOG	Parliamentary Forum on Oil and Gas (Uganda)
RAC	Royal African Company
SEC	Securities and Exchange Commission (USA)
SIGAR	Special Inspector General for Afghanistan Reconstruction (USA)
SWHAP	Swedish Workplace HIV/AIDS Programme
UN	United Nations
UNCTAD	United Nations Conference on Trade and Development
UNDESA	United Nations Department of Economic and Social Affairs
UNDP	United Nations Development Programme
UNEP	United Nations Environment Programme
UNESCO	United Nations Educational, Scientific and Cultural Organization
UNGA	United Nations General Assembly
UNGC	United Nations Global Compact
UNICEF	United Nations Children's Fund
UNITA	National Union for the Total Independence of Angola
Unocal	United Oil of California
UNODC	United Nations Office on Drugs and Crime
UNSC	United Nations Security Council
USAID	United States Agency for International Development
WEF	World Economic Forum
WHO	World Health Organization
WGC	World Gold Council
WTO	World Trade Organization
WWF	World Wide Fund for Nature
ZAPSO	Zimbabwe AIDS Prevention and Support Organisation

Business and conflict in fragile states

In October 2006, Ugandan president Yoweri Museveni announced the confirmation of commercial-quality oil reserves in Uganda's Albertine Graben region, attracting the immediate attention of international companies who by 2009 had invested over US$700 million in exploration.[1] Commercial production of recoverable reserves estimated to be well above the one billion barrel mark is anticipated to begin by 2017 or 2018.[2] With oil operations a potentially important source of government revenues, jobs and economic growth, the assertion is that oil will, as stated by the president during the run-up to the 2016 elections, 'help us transform the country'.[3] Contributions of oil exploitation to peaceful development would be a critical positive achievement in a country with a per capita GDP below US$700 in 2014, and where measures of sustainable economic opportunity, welfare and education seem stuck or are trending downwards.[4]

Yet communities blockade oil company operations, protesting against forced removals from communal lands and the hiring of non-Ugandans as truck drivers.[5] Traditional authorities fight with the national government, with the king of Bunyoro – the titular head of a regional government in the west of Uganda – appearing unannounced in parliament to demand a greater share of oil royalties for local communities, a greater voice in decisions for communities and protection from violence tied to development activities.[6] Rival groups fight with each other for the control of land they believe will benefit from oil exploitation, resulting in scores of deaths, while even fishermen who had long coexisted across the Democratic Republic of the Congo (DRC)-Uganda border now feel compelled to defend their territory from one another.

The politics of oil unfold in an atmosphere of substantial tension and fear. The Albertine Graben region follows the country's border with the DRC and has South Sudan as its northern limit. Ugandan local districts that overlap with the oil resources in the country's impoverished north have been an arena for many of the region's conflicts, from colonial-era troubles through Uganda's civil wars to the ongoing insurgency by the Lord's Resistance Army against the current government.[7] The national intelligence infrastructure monitors non-governmental organisations (NGOs), acting with particular aggression towards 'activity that could threaten government and private company investments' by stopping meetings, detaining NGO members and accusing them of 'economic sabotage'.[8] Bishops in this highly religious country raised issues of justice, only to be told by the president to rather attend to baptisms.[9] Whereas the World Bank had noted improvements in Ugandan governance from 1986, since the confirmation of exploitable oil resources in 2006 measures of voice and accountability, regulatory quality, control of corruption and rule of law are trending negatively.[10] Just as ominously, a coordinated attack in 2014 on 13 government installations including police stations and an army base in the oil-rich districts of Kasese, Bundibugyo and Ntororo, killing 90 people, recalls the oil-producing region's dark history since the country's independence.[11]

As conflict escalates and an already complex environment becomes perhaps even more fragile, some companies are accused of exploiting the country's weak rule of law and divisive politics for economic gain. Others, such as Tullow Oil, find that they cannot realise their own objectives, and so reduce their stakes in the country and seek opportunities elsewhere.[12] With the promised sustainable business profitability or social outcomes nowhere to be seen, so far the main by-product of the intense wave of foreign investment in oil exploration and development appears to be conflict, often enough violent.

New lenses on business and conflict in fragile states

This book is about conflict related to large-scale investments in fragile states like Uganda. It is written for the global enterprise that seeks to manage conflict risks and help create a stable operating environment; the government that hopes to deliver on the promise of private-sector development as an engine of inclusive growth; the multilateral institution or development agency that is frustrated by lack of progress in reducing fragility and is searching for new strategies to implement the 2030 Agenda for Sustainable Development; and the advocates who question whether foreign companies can play a role in peaceful development for communities at all. It explores why the 'win–win' promise of private-sector jobs, tax revenues, and economic growth to help lift a fragile country out of poverty and instability often enough becomes a story of lost opportunity for businesses, communities, peacebuilders and good governance advocates alike as a result of persistent and often violent conflict. In particular, the book takes a hard look at the international policy regime for business and conflict in fragile states: both the initiatives to regulate, control and hold to account multinational enterprises that profit from, or become complicit in, conflict and violence; and the attempts to create a strong legal and institutional framework to facilitate an expanded private-sector role in peaceful development.

Its conclusions are straightforward. Both sustainable business and inclusive growth require stability, underpinned by broadly legitimate institutions, the effective recognition of human rights, an enabling environment for human enterprise, and the rule of law. The aims of international policy at an aspirational level are therefore not subject to critique. But international focus on multinational companies as the lever for change – whether by restraining or unleashing them – fails to account for the changing dynamics of conflict and violence in fragile states. These can be summarised as an evolution from the pre-eminence of inter- and intra-state armed conflict to a more complex world of conflict and violence. In this new strategic landscape, multinational enterprises may indeed sometimes cause conflict more or less directly; but more often their operations are one set of stress factors among many – including environmental change, rapid urbanisation, political fragmentation, a demographic shift towards youth, the growth of transnational criminal networks, and others – that in aggregate result in destructive conflict or violence.

Effective policy must therefore address the entire conflict system, not just the company. The international rule of law and state-building agendas for fragile states aspire to address systemic issues, but 'basic governance transformations may take 20–40 years'.[13] All the while, conflicts related to large-scale business operations in fragile states that are endemic, increasing in number, and in many places growing in intensity undermine both business and social goals – including the good governance agenda itself. The ability to manage the acute conflicts of today and the many outbreaks of violence that can be anticipated tomorrow thus remains beyond the reach of contemporary international policy on business and conflict.

What is needed are solutions to business and conflict in fragile states that can be implemented successfully in the reasonably immediate term. They should be able to succeed despite the constraints of fragile environments themselves – including weak institutions, lack of trust in government, legacies of abuse by economic actors, or spoilers in the form of company managers, government officials or rebel leaders content to use, or at least tolerate, conflict and violence to meet their narrowly defined goals. Recognising the essentially local nature of both business operations and of conflict and violence, effective approaches must also be responsive to the particular social, political, economic and conflict dynamics among a specific set of actors in a particular time and place.

What may be surprising to those focused more narrowly on private-sector actors and approaches is that such solutions exist. The solutions are well enough established in the realms of peacebuilding, conflict prevention and violence reduction to be broadly considered mainstream. They are underpinned by reasonably well-articulated principles and well-understood mechanisms of action. Furthermore, the available evidence from emerging business practice suggests that these solutions – based on strong analysis, engagement of progressively larger coalitions for change, and iterative, well-monitored actions – can also be applied to prevent and manage conflicts in the context of large-scale business investments. The book concludes that it is indeed possible to put the promises of 'security, justice and jobs'[14] together to mitigate conflict and ultimately reduce fragility. This will not happen through a process of syndicating and then implementing universal norms from the international to the national levels in fragile states, however, but rather through pragmatic and holistic approaches implemented at the local level.

The rising tide of business and conflict

Companies, multilateral institutions, donor governments, and even some development and peacebuilding NGOs argue that large-scale foreign direct investment (FDI) should be a boon for Uganda and other fragile states. Such states can be defined as those particularly susceptible to crisis, associated with government failures to provide security, economic opportunity or rule of law to significant proportions of its citizens, and with institutional structures that may reinforce rather than mitigate conflict.[15] Multinational enterprises enter fragile contexts with promises of jobs, infusion of capital, technical know-how and training, linkages to global markets, value chain development, best practices for managing social, environmental, and labour issues, and some influence with fragile state governments. It is therefore hoped that FDI can 'generate the kind of economic development which both addresses the underlying economic dimensions of conflict and also provides for the urgent priorities of creating jobs and ensuring basic services are delivered to the population'.[16] The provision of jobs and services may in turn reduce socio-political tensions in ways that create space for consensus-building and practical progress on security, civil rights, good government and other challenges.[17] Given the reinforcing dynamics of economic hardship, grievance and political rivalry present in fragile states, the economic and broader social benefits of large-scale investments are therefore held out as one way of helping to cut the Gordian knot of fragility.

Yet over the last two decades, confrontations among companies, communities and governments in fragile states related to large-scale business operations have been growing in number and intensity. In Guatemala, right-wing paramilitary forces are implicated in violence, including killings and gang rapes, against opponents to Canadian and Guatemalan mining interests; in Zimbabwe, government forces reacted violently towards the 20,000 victims of flooding from the Tokwe-Mukorsi Dam (constructed by an Italian industrial group) who opposed plans to resettle them on government-supported sugar cane plantations; in Indonesia, a Singapore-based agribusiness company is alleged to have acted in concert with local police to destroy indigenous villages in order to establish palm oil plantations; in Malaysia, a blockade by villagers to stop the construction of the Baram Dam enters its second year; in Peru, community groups have halted the development of Newmont Mining Corporation's multibillion-dollar Conga copper and gold project; and in Liberia, projects to boost the export agriculture sector are dramatically behind the timeline agreed to by industry and government because of conflicts with communities over land acquisition and compensation.[18]

These are not isolated incidents. A review of the lowest-ranking 100 countries on the Fragile States Index shows that virtually all have confronted significant, and often deadly, conflict in connection with large-scale business investments in the past five years.[19] Such deadly conflict can range, for instance, from illicit trade in natural resources in war-ridden Central Africa to more isolated deaths related to protests over mine operator Barrick Gold Corporation's Pueblo Viejo project in the relatively stable Dominican Republic.[20]

Push and pushback in fragile states

This increase in destructive conflict related to large-scale business operations, characterised by protest, upheaval and violence, is explained by a number of dynamics. By the 1990s, it was broadly understood that a global corporation could not ignore the opportunities represented by less-developed countries,[21] and companies found that they could find there higher returns despite instability.[22] Countries such as Colombia, Indonesia, Algeria and the Philippines attracted high levels of FDI even during periods of overt armed conflict;[23] flows of FDI to Côte d'Ivoire remained positive during the entire civil war.[24] Countries like Brazil, South Africa and Mexico also highlight that FDI occurs despite high levels of criminal violence.[25] Companies also look for first-mover advantages in newly opened markets such as Myanmar, or those just emerging from conflict such as the DRC or the Balkans, and benefit from government incentives to be on the leading edge of investment in still-unstable places such as Afghanistan and Iraq. As *The Economist* noted in 2000, 'For brave businessfolk, there are rich pickings in grim places'.[26]

Both exogenous and endogenous factors are at play here. The former include the rise of Asia and a resulting scramble for available agricultural lands. According to one advocacy organisation, 'More than 81 million acres of land worldwide – an area the size of Portugal – has been sold off to foreign investors'.[27] At the same time, mining 'has moved from developed to emerging economies ... Huge investments have taken place in Latin America, Africa, and parts of Asia and these are likely to escalate in the next ten years.'[28] The latter include the need for infrastructure in fragile states, leading the World Bank to advocate, for example, the doubling of investments in Africa for dams, roads, railways and ports.[29]

These factors add up to the more than US$700bn in FDI in developing economies across Africa, Latin America, and Asia in 2014, representing 56% of global FDI flows; as one example, FDI doubled year on year in highly fragile Myanmar.[30] Additionally, under Chinese leadership, the Asian Infrastructure Investment Bank will lend money for road, mobile phone and other infrastructure projects for Asian countries.[31] Conflict in the context of large-scale business investments is on the rise in part because of the trend of international capital increasingly migrating to more conflict-prone environments.

At the same time, pushback to these investments is likely to increase. Many fragile states exhibit growing populist wariness towards Western economic models and an increasingly globalised economy. The disconnect between economic liberalisation and GDP growth on the one hand and broad-based improvements in quality of life on the other has not gone unnoticed. Zambia's per capita GDP of US$1,722, driven by investments in the extractives sector, for example, is roughly twice that of neighbouring Zimbabwe (US$896)[32] – yet 57% of the population in Zambia live in poverty as defined by the Multidimensional Poverty Index, compared to 30% in Zimbabwe.[33] In the agricultural sector, a European Union-funded guide notes that 'Increasing global demands for food and biofuels are resulting in foreign governments and big companies buying or leasing millions of hectares of land in Africa … in 'land grabs', so-called because of the human rights abuses that often occur when such land is acquired';[34] the UN special rapporteur on the right to food asserted flatly that 'The current food systems are efficient only from the point of view of maximizing agribusiness profits.'[35]

A complex landscape of fragility

Such perceptions fuel a neo-colonial narrative in which the foreign corporation is a familiar enemy. 'There could hardly be a more effective form of colonialism,' stated Dr Tewolde Egziabher, head of the African Group and Like-Minded Group of Developing Countries in the negotiations toward the Cartagena Protocol on biosafety, in relation to the opening of emerging markets for proprietary seeds of American and European companies. 'The genetic engineering industry will effectively be able to hold us hostage.'[36]

Formerly monolithic government structures show signs of unravelling in many places. Parties such as the African

National Congress in South Africa that formerly represented the people's revolution find themselves attacked from the left, with calls by the newly formed Economic Freedom Fighters for the nationalisation of mines and expropriation of land without compensation, characterised as 'resistance against colonial and economic domination and exploitation'[37] and backed up by confrontational tactics at the national and local levels. Emergent human rights concepts such as the requirement of 'free, prior and informed consent'[38] by indigenous peoples to the use of their land – whatever the views of their national governments – as well as heightened environmental sensibilities, create rallying points for popular mobilisation and international support. Furthermore, technology has changed the calculus of protest and upheaval by enabling links between like-minded groups across developing countries, and between opponents of multinational corporations in fragile environments and their allies in Western capitals.

Conflict in the context of large-scale business investment is therefore on the rise also because of deep divisions in how international capital is perceived and responded to in complex environments. With both the shift towards more investment in fragile states and the emergent opposition to the perceived excesses of liberalisation and globalisation being growing trends, we can expect that there will be more business-related conflict in fragile states in the future.

These tensions and stress factors associated with large-scale investment in fragile states in turn interact with pre-existing conflict systems. The drivers of conflict dynamics differ from place to place. They may be socio-economic, including high unemployment, food shortages, rapid urbanisation, low levels of education, labour unrest or high levels of inequality. They may be socio-political, including ethnic or religious competition, inter-regional or regional–national tensions, real or perceived discrimination, unresolved grievances or pronounced disagreements over the role of the state. They may be governance and justice challenges, including severe corruption, human rights abuses, lack of a functioning legal system, or inconsistent or erratic government decision-making. They may be security challenges, including armed conflict, regional instability, a legacy of violence or trauma, criminal networks, high levels of violent crime, terrorism or challenges for demobilised combatants.

At the same time, fragile states are characterised by a diminished capacity to manage tensions and stress factors in a complex environment. Challenges can include lack of government legitimacy in the eyes of significant segments of the population or deep distrust in the aftermath of conflict.[39] The ability of different political and social groups to reach consensus or resolve disputes can also be diminished by a variety of pressures. These comprise demographic trends, such as population growth and rapid urbanisation; power shifts among political factions and between state and non-state actors; climate change, including more natural disasters and climatic fluctuations; and new conflict dynamics, including geopolitical tension and more chronic violence.[40] Pre-existing conflict dynamics in which multinational corporations become entwined, diminished government capacity and legitimacy, and stresses on conflict resolution systems mean that large-scale investments in mining, agriculture or infrastructure projects in fragile states will occur in the context of a heightened risk of conflict and violence.

The business case for better management of business and conflict

Increasingly, the evidence of the direct cost to business of such conflict is incontrovertible. Unmanaged and unmitigated conflict risks can lead to fatalities and injuries, lapses in safety, destruction of assets, operational disruptions, project abandonment and management distraction from business issues. A study of direct costs to business of company–community conflicts found one nine-month construction delay that resulted in US$750m in additional project costs. Stoppages at another company's project carried a price tag of US$100m per year, and a community's ability to protest against a third company by cutting its power lines cost it US$750,000 per day. Of 50 company conflicts surveyed, more than a third involved at least one fatality.[41] Platinum group metals producer Lonmin PLC saw its share price drop 30% within a week of the 2012 massacre of workers protesting at its Marikana platinum mine, the protests linked to long-standing tensions between the company, rival labour unions, local government and communities.[42] A subsequent five-month industry-wide strike cost Lonmin, Anglo American Platinum and Impala Platinum a combined US$2.25bn in lost revenues.[43]

When conflict and violence are turned against a company – whether for political or criminal ends – it can also be costly to protect against these factors. Oil firms in Algeria have been estimated to allocate 9% of their operational budgets to security, while a small business in Jamaica may spend 17% of revenues.[44] And, in a world where business increasingly looks to emerging markets for growth and profitability, costs to business must also be measured in delayed market entry and lost opportunities.

Markets increasingly understand and account for these risks and dynamics. One study found that the value of the gold in the ground now represents as little as 22% of the market valuation of a gold company; socio-political support for or opposition to the company's mines, in contrast, may represent from 45% to as much as 65% of the company's share value.[45]

The social costs of business and conflict are also high. Over 1bn people, including about 340m of the world's extreme poor, live in the 50 most fragile states.[46] Additionally, 'the gap between fragile, violence-affected countries and other developing countries is widening'; conflict-affected and fragile states 'are the furthest away from achieving the Millennium Development Goals'.[47] By 2030, 'poverty could become increasingly concentrated in fragile states: even under the best-case scenario, 62% of the global poor will be located in fragile states'. This may include as many as 500m people living on less than US$1.25 per day.[48] State fragility is also 'linked with a range of transnational security threats and humanitarian concerns, including mass migration, organized crime, violent conflict, communicable diseases, environmental degradation and, more recently, terrorism'.[49] This deprivation and conflict have a strongly local component: marginalised neighbourhoods have been found to be flashpoints for violence in cities;[50] poorer regions within the same country may also be more prone to conflict.[51]

At the same time, measured voices such as that of Harvard economics professor and Nobel laureate Amartya Sen remind us that 'no economy in world history has ever achieved widespread prosperity, going beyond the high life of the elite, without making considerable use of markets'.[52] To the extent that a vigorous and inclusive private sector can play a role in providing broad-based hope and opportunity, fragility should be reduced. But when business causes, exacerbates or is drawn into conflicts in fragile states, peacebuilding and development opportunities are lost, social expectations remain unmet, trust is undermined, narratives of conflict continue, and the dynamics of fragility are reinforced. Until the interrelated dynamics of business, conflict and development can be managed in fragile states, there is little prospect for raising the global poor out of poverty.

A new logic for business risk mitigation and conflict prevention

In contemporary international discourse, the assertion that large-scale foreign investments can help reduce fragility has confronted the reality of global corporations becoming embroiled in fragile state conflict and violence. This has of late sparked significant international attention: from the World Bank's review of the link between conflict and development in its *World Development Report 2011: Conflict, Security and Development*; to the adoption of the Guiding Principles on Business and Human Rights by the UN Human Rights Council also in 2011; to successes and frustrations in litigation against multinational businesses in US and European courts; to changes in development and peacebuilding policies to favour private-sector solutions from Colombia to Myanmar; and many other initiatives.

This book explores these contemporary international responses to business and conflict in fragile states: their histories and underlying premises, how they may be helping, where they are falling short and what might be done about it by multinational corporations and others. The book starts from the premise that corrosive conflict has high costs for companies, governments and communities alike, undermining their interests and aspirations. It argues that new approaches are not only called for, but also available by turning to mainstream peacebuilding and conflict prevention practice applied to the private-sector arena.

The book's focus on 'fragile states' recognises that state capacities and functions are challenged in many regions of the world. Governments in the capital may not exercise complete territorial control, and in many cases state control is contested or resisted at national, regional or local levels. States that fail to provide people with security, welfare and representation often lack government legitimacy.[53] Such states and societies are encountering 'fragile situations', defined by the World Bank as representing 'periods when states or institutions lack the capacity, accountability, or legitimacy to mediate relations between citizen groups and between citizens and the state, making them vulnerable to violence'.[54] In fragile states, the structures of government tend to reinforce rather than mitigate dynamics of conflict and violence.[55]

The focus of this book is particularly on 'large footprint' investments in fragile states. The measure is not necessarily the size of an enterprise or the scale of the investment, but rather the extent of its impact on the ground. The companies in question, such as those in the extractives industries, agriculture or infrastructure development, inevitably become entangled with, and part of, broader systems and dynamics that create and maintain fragility. The book emphasises the sharp edge of business and conflict, characterised by heightened inter-group tension, community protests and labour unrest, political upheaval, increased criminality, or heavy-handed responses by besieged governments, all of which increase the risk of violence; it looks at those situations where the promised 'win–win' for business and development has instead manifested 'lose–lose' outcomes.[56]

In its first two chapters, the book explores the two dominant contemporary discourses on business and conflict in fragile states, tracing their sources and surveying their expressions in contemporary international policy.

Chapter One explores the view of the multinational corporation as a cause of conflict and violence in fragile states. It shows how NGOs concerned with democratisation and development, international human rights bodies, accountability advocates and others draw on an enduring legacy of global enterprises willing to exploit fragile conditions, strike deals with unsavoury actors, and foment conflict for economic gain; in this context, multinational corporations are seen as fundamentally profit-hungry, soulless and seemingly stateless. The chapter explores the logical extension of this perspective, namely advocacy for a variety of legal-regulatory approaches to contain the worst forms of corporate conduct in fragile states, both through legal accountability in the companies' home countries and through international regulation.

Chapter Two explores the competing view of the multinational corporation as a force for conflict reduction in fragile states. It shows how multilateral financial institutions, growth-oriented fragile state governments, business advocates and others draw on an almost equally long-standing liberal economic history to understand a vigorous and inclusive private sector as the foundation for peaceful development. The chapter explores state-building approaches that support the regulation of an open economy and the protection of private-sector interests, as well as advocacy for ever-greater roles for multinational corporations in fragile state affairs. The analysis concludes that these two dominant discourses concerning business and conflict in fragile states have few points of intersection and exist largely in tension with one another.

The book then analyses why these contemporary international responses have not added up in any systematic way to successful management of business and conflict in fragile states, whether defined as the containment of corporate wrongdoing or the establishment of a firmer private-sector foundation for peaceful development.

Chapter Three starts with the recognition that both dominant international policy frameworks put the international corporation at the centre of the story, the main difference being whether the global corporation is described as hero or villain. Both frameworks draw on understandings of conflict rooted in inter-state and civil warfare, and the role of companies within them. This chapter widens the lens on business and conflict to describe a changing landscape of conflict and violence in fragile states. It examines both local factors such as urbanisation, the infiltration of criminal networks and the fragmentation of political power, as well as more global factors such as environmental change and geopolitical tension to which fragile states may be particularly sensitive. It concludes that the contemporary international focus on the behaviour of multinational corporations – and in particular those within reach of multilateral financial institutions and Western policymakers – is inadequate to address the many intertwined dynamics of business and conflict in fragile states. A variety of critical actors – from multinational companies from the Global South to traditional authorities in conflict with national governments – are left out of the equation; and even a company that achieved compliance with international regulatory requirements and emerging social responsibility norms could not, on that basis, ensure a stable operating environment free of destructive conflict.

Chapter Four takes as its starting point the time frames required for desired changes in the dynamics of business and conflict in fragile states under the dominant international policy regimes now being pursued. The chapter notes that the impacts of state-building, microeconomic responses to macro-economic transformation and legal/regulatory reform are typically measured in decades, if not generations. Furthermore, contemporary approaches appear to largely ignore the political economy of fragile states themselves, in effect exhorting them to be less fragile by adopting the trappings of the Western liberal state. It concludes that attempted reforms will at best only deliver their intended results in the long term – and at worst, the ways in which reforms are now being pursued in many places will exacerbate conflict. Taking these factors together, the analysis concludes that contemporary international policy responses to business and conflict in fragile states – however important they may turn out to be for the long haul – will remain seriously hampered in their attempts to address the underlying drivers of risk and conflict in difficult places in the short to medium term.

The book then explores alternatives to the dominant international approaches that could perhaps better address destructive conflicts related to large-scale business operations in fragile states as they unfold today and can be anticipated to increase in number and intensity tomorrow.

Chapter Five looks outside the private sector for inspiration. It draws from mainstream peacebuilding and conflict prevention practice in areas as diverse as electoral conflicts and urban violence reduction to demonstrate that even acute conflict is preventable and manageable. The chapter notes that successful conflict mitigation strategies in highly complex environments share common principles and approaches, and well-understood mechanisms of action. Examining available evidence from the private sector, it shows that these principles and practices, when applied to the corporate domain, can be predicted to have the same positive impacts. It concludes that solutions are there, but are to be found largely outside the current debates about either regulation or enablement of the private sector; conflict and violence are their own phenomena and need to be dealt with on their own terms. The analysis underlines that, in order to be effective, international policies must address not only the 'what' of better approaches to business and conflict, but also the 'how' of implementation in fragile contexts that have frustrated state-building and regulatory approaches alike. The chapter explores how promising approaches can be applied in fragmented and even hostile political environments. It concludes that progress is most quickly and dependably achieved by focusing on localised solutions that address the currently perceived risks and future aspirations of the broadest possible range of stakeholders.

The book concludes that neither company shareholders nor advocates for peaceful development need, or should, accept the growing cost of business-related conflict in fragile environments. It is unhelpfully naïve to ignore the actors inside and outside companies and governments who are perfectly willing to profit from fragile state dynamics, including violence; but it is irresponsibly cynical to ignore the increasingly strong evidence of conflict mitigation strategies that all the same work.

The analysis that follows therefore steers clear of any attempt to play referee between the dominant, competing contemporary international discourses on the private sector in fragile states – it finds ample evidence that the story of the predatory company and the story of the healthy private sector as one foundation for peaceful development both are true and both are incomplete. Neither does the book in any way argue against continuing efforts to pursue justice, human rights or an enabling environment for an inclusive and sustainable economy through institutional and legal reform – it simply notes that rule-of-law and state-building approaches are unlikely to provide solutions to conflict on the ground any time soon, and that the failure to address festering conflict with greater urgency will undermine these laudable goals.

The book rather argues that international policy debates caught up in old ways of looking at business, conflict and fragility are for the most part ignoring violence reduction and conflict management approaches that can mitigate today's conflicts. Moving pragmatism to the fore, the book concludes that those who want to provide positive leadership on business and conflict in fragile states – whether businesses looking for sustainable profitability, advocates seeking greater positive impact for vulnerable populations, or international institutions seeking reduced fragility and inclusive development – have much work to do, but many places to start.

Notes

1   Petrus de Kock and Kathryn Sturman, *The Power of Oil: Charting Uganda's Transition to a Petro-State* (Johannesburg: South African Institute of International Affairs, 2012), p. 8.

2   Paul Tentena, 'Uganda Set for 2018 Oil Mark', *East African Business Week*, 21 June 2014.

3   Frederic Musisi, 'Who Will Manage Uganda's Oil Better?', *Daily Monitor* (Kampala), 3 January 2016.

4   Mo Ibrahim Foundation, *2015 Ibrahim Index of African Governance: Country Insights – Uganda* (London: Mo Ibrahim Foundation, 2015), p. 4, available at http://data.worldbank.org/indicator/NY.GDP.PCAP.CD.

5   Unless otherwise noted, information in this section is based on interviews by Brian Ganson in Uganda in 2012.

6   Henry Sekanjako, 'Bunyoro King Storms Parliament Over Oil Revenue', *New Vision*, 1 June 2012.

7   Ogengu Otunnu, 'The Conflict in Northern Uganda: Causes and Consequences', in Okello Lucima (ed.), *Protracted Conflict, Elusive Peace: Initiatives to End the Violence in Northern Uganda* (London: Conciliation Resources, 2002), pp. 10–13.

8   Human Rights Watch, *Curtailing Criticism: Intimidation and Obstruction of Civil Society in Uganda* (New York: Human Rights Watch, 2012), p. 3.

9   Brian Ganson, *Risk and Risk Mitigation in the Oil and Gas Sector in Uganda* (Geneva: Geneva Peacebuilding Platform, 2012).

10 See data for the years 2006–2014, Worldwide Governance Indicators, *Country Data Report for Uganda, 1996–2014* (Washington, DC: World Bank, 2015), available at http://info.worldbank.org/governance/wgi/index.aspx#countryReports.

11 Patrick Kagenda, 'Behind the Attacks in Western Uganda', *Independent*, 28 July 2014.

12 Selina Williams, 'Tullow May Sell Part of Stake in Ugandan Oil Field', *Wall Street Journal*, 12 February 2015.

13 Organisation for Economic Co-operation and Development (OECD), *A New Deal for Engagement in Fragile States* (Paris: OECD, 2011), p. 1.

14 World Bank, *World Development Report 2011: Conflict, Security and Development* (Washington, DC: World Bank, 2011), p. xii.

15 For a review of definitions of 'fragile states', see Achim Wennmann, *Grasping the Strengths of Fragile States: Aid Effectiveness between 'Top-down' and 'Bottom-up' Statebuilding*, CCDP Working Paper 6 (Geneva: The Graduate Institute, 2010), pp. 15–20. For a review of the fragile states debate, see James Putzel and Jonathan Di John, *Meeting the Challenges of Crisis States: Crisis States Research Centre Report* (London:

London School of Economics, 2012); and the special issue 'Fragile States: A Political Concept', *Third World Quarterly*, vol. 35, no. 2, March 2014.

16 Canan Gündüz and Charlotte Vaillant, *Addressing the Economic Dimensions of Peacebuilding Through Trade and Support to Private Enterprise* (London: International Alert, 2006), p. 3.

17 World Bank, *World Development Report 2011*.

18 Examples draw on Business and Human Rights Resource Center Database, http://business-humanrights.org.

19 Based on the authors' comparison of the 100 most fragile states as reported in the Fragile States Index (http://fsi.fundforpeace.org) and at least one known example of deadly conflict relating to a large-scale investment site in each fragile state from 2010–2015.

20 United Nations Office on Drugs and Crime (UNODC), *Organized Crime and Instability in Central Africa: A Threat Assessment*. (Vienna: UNODC, 2011). 'Mining in the Dominican Republic: Sickness and Wealth', *The Economist*, 21 September 2013.

21 Virginia Haufler, *Dangerous Commerce: Insurance and the Management of International Risk* (Ithaca, NY: Cornell University Press, 1997).

22 Tricia Goulbourne, *Corporate Social Responsibility: The Business Case* (Ontario: Carleton University, 2003).

23 Ashley Campbell, *The Private Sector and Conflict Prevention Mainstreaming* (Ontario: Country Indicators for Foreign Policy, 2002).

24 Multilateral Investment Guarantee Agency (MIGA), *World Investment and Political Risk 2010* (Washington, DC: MIGA, 2010), pp. 28–50.

25 Achim Wennmann, 'The Role of Business in Armed Violence Reduction and Prevention', *International Review of the Red Cross*, vol. 94, no. 887, 2011, pp. 919–40, at pp. 925–6.

26 'Risky Returns: Business in Difficult Places', *The Economist*, 20 May 2000.

27 Oxfam America, 'The Truth About Land Grabs', see http://www.oxfamamerica. org/take-action/campaign/ food-farming-and-hunger/ land-grabs.

28 International Council on Mining and Metals (ICMM), *Trends in the Mining and Metals Industry* (London: ICMM, 2012), pp. 5–6.

29 Vivien Foster and Cecilia Briceno-Garmendia (eds), *Africa's Infrastructure: A Time for Transformation* (Washington, DC: World Bank, 2010).

30 United Nations Conference on Trade and Development (UNCTAD), *Global Investment Trends Monitor No. 18* (Geneva: UNCTAD, 2015).

31 'Why China is Creating a New "World Bank" for Asia', *The Economist*, 11 November 2014.

32 World Bank data for 2014. See http:// data.worldbank.org/indicator/ NY.GDP.PCAP.CD.

33 Oxford Poverty and Human Development Initiative, Global Multidimensional Poverty Index Databank. OPHI, University of Oxford. December 2015 data.

34 Janet Pritchard, Feja Lesniewska, Tom Lomax, Saskia Ozinga and Cynthia Morel, *Securing Community*

Land and Resource Rights in Africa: A Guide to Legal Reform and Best Practices (Brussels, Moreton in Marsh, London and Yaoundé: FERN, Forest Peoples Programme, ClientEarth, and Centre for Environment and Development, 2013), p. 9.

35 Office of the United Nations High Commissioner for Human Rights (OHCHR), 'Democracy and Diversity Can Mend Broken Food Systems: Final Diagnosis from UN Right to Food Expert', presse release, 10 March 2014, available at http://www.ohchr.org/EN/NewsEvents/Pages/DisplayNews.aspx?NewsID=14336&LangID=E.

36 Interview with Dr Tewolde Egziabher by Michael Friedrich of Greenpeace, http://www.greenpeace.org/international/en/campaigns/agriculture/problem/genetic-engineering/feeding-the-world-facts-vers/risks.

37 Economic Freedom Fighters Founding Manifesto, 27 July 2013, available at http://effighters.org.za/documents/economic-freedom-fighters-founding-manifesto.

38 United Nations General Assembly (UNGA), United Nations Declaration on the Rights of Indigenous Peoples: resolution/ adopted by the General Assembly, 2 October 2007, A/RES/61/295.

39 Brian Ganson, 'How Do We Succeed in a Complex Environment?', in Brian Ganson (ed.), *Management in Complex Environments: Questions for Leaders* (Stockholm: International Council of Swedish Industry, 2013), pp. 10–16.

40 National Intelligence Council (NIC), *Global Trends 2030: Alternative Worlds* (Washington, DC: NIC, 2012); Martin Commission for Future Generations, *Now for the Long Term* (Oxford: University of Oxford, 2013); Jerome C. Glenn, Theodore J. Gordon, and Elizabeth Florescu, *State of the Future 2013–2014* (Washington, DC: The Millennium Project, 2014).

41 Daniel M. Franks, Rachel Davis, Anthony J. Bebbington, Saleem H. Ali, Deanna Kemp, and Martin Scurrah, 'Conflict Translates Environmental and Social Risk into Business Costs', *Proceedings of the National Academy of Sciences of the United States of America*, vol. 111, no. 21 (2014), pp. 7576–81.

42 Fifi Peters, 'Lonmin Recuperates After Marikana Tragedy', *Business Day Live*, 19 Aug 2013.

43 Ed Stoddard, 'South Africa Miners Return to Work After Longest Platinum Strike', Reuters, 25 June 2014.

44 Peter W. Singer, *Corporate Warriors: The Rise of the Privatized Military Industry* (Ithaca, NY: Cornell University Press, 2003), pp. 81–2. United Nations Office on Drugs and Crime (UNODC) and World Bank, *Crime, Violence, and Development: Trends, Costs and Policy Options in the Caribbean* (Vienna and Washington, DC: UNODC and World Bank, 2007), pp. 48–49.

45 Witold J. Henisz, Sinziana Dorobantu, and Lite Nartey Henisz, 'Spinning Gold: The Financial and Operational Returns to External Stakeholder Engagement', *Strategic Management Journal*, vol. 35, no. 12, 2014, pp. 1727–48.

46 Paul Collier, *The Bottom Billion: Why the Poorest Countries are Failing and*

What Can Be Done About It (Oxford: Oxford University Press, 2007).

47 OECD, *A New Deal for Engagement in Fragile States*, p. 1.

48 OECD, *States of Fragility: Meeting Post-2015 Ambitions* (Paris: OECD, 2015), p. 21.

49 Claire Mcloughlin, *Topic Guide on Fragile States* (Birmingham: Governance and Social Development Resource Centre, 2012), p. 8.

50 Small Arms Survey, *Small Arms Survey 2007: Guns and the City* (Cambridge: Cambridge University Press, 2007), pp. 175–6.

51 Ejaz Ghani and Lakshmi Iyer, 'Conflict and Development: Lessons from South Asia', *Economic Premise No. 31* (Washington, DC: World Bank, 2010).

52 Amartya Sen, *Identity and Violence* (New York: WW Norton & Co., 2006), p. 137.

53 OECD, *Supporting Statebuilding in Situations of Conflict and Fragility: Policy Guidance* (Paris: OECD, 2011).

54 World Bank, *World Development Report 2011*, p. xvi.

55 Robert H. Bates, *When Things Fell Apart: State Failure in Late-Century Africa* (Cambridge: Cambridge University Press, 2008), pp. 129–30.

56 The understanding of 'conflict' in this book is rooted in conflict resolution and transformation theory and practice. See, for instance, Johan Galtung, *Peace By Peaceful Means: Peace and Conflict, Development and Civilization* (Oslo: International Peace Research Institute, 1996); Friedrich Glasl, 'The Process of Conflict Escalation and Roles of Third Parties', in Gerard B.J. Bomers and Richard B. Peterson (eds), *Conflict Management and Industrial Relations* (The Hague: Kluwer Nijhoff Publishing, 1982), pp. 119–40; Jay Folberg and Alison Taylor, *Mediation: A Comprehensive Guide to Resolving Conflict Without Litigation* (San Francisco, CA: Jossey-Bass Publishers, 1984), pp. 18–37.

CHAPTER ONE

Predatory companies in fragile states

The Dutch East India Company is generally regarded as the world's first modern multinational corporation. Having executed its initial public offering – a global first – in 1602, it grew to operate a diversified portfolio of commercial interests including agribusiness, transport, manufacturing and brewing.

The company was also a brutally violent enterprise. In 1621 Jan Pieterszoon Coen, an accountant who became the company's governor-general, used Japanese mercenaries to behead and quarter indigenous leaders as part of his campaign to control the nutmeg production of Great Banda, an island of present-day Indonesia. This was after having used a naval blockade to starve the population into submission. Coen then sold some 14,000 indigenous inhabitants of the island into slavery to replace them with non-native slave labour that could more easily be controlled. In 1629 he ordered the beheading of ten English rivals to put a final end to the English East India Company's spice operations in the area. This he did despite the instructions from his board, the Council of Seventeen, that he must cooperate with the English on terms agreed to between the two companies, rather than fight them. One officer of the

Dutch East India Company wrote that 'things are carried on in such a criminal and murderous way that the blood of the poor people cries to heaven for revenge'.[1]

Jumping forward some 350 years, DiamondWorks Ltd is a Canadian company that was successful in negotiating concession agreements with regimes in Angola and Sierra Leone during those countries' vicious civil wars in the 1990s. Executive Outcomes was a private military company founded in 1989 by Eeben Barlow, formerly of the South African Defence Force. He had served in 32 Battalion, which was responsible for destabilising South Africa's neighbours through sabotage and support for rebel movements. Barlow had also been a regional coordinator for the South African Civil Cooperation Bureau, one of the apartheid government's units with specific responsibility for acts of arson, intimidation, sabotage and murder against its enemies. DiamondWorks and Executive Outcomes shared offices in London, as well as a major shareholder, Anthony Buckingham.

Buckingham had reached agreement with the Angolan government for Executive Outcomes to lead operations to reclaim the port of Soyo in Angola, overrun by National Union for the Total Independence of Angola (UNITA) rebels in 1993. Soyo was an operating base for foreign oil companies, including Ranger Oil West Africa Ltd, in which Buckingham's Heritage Oil (itself formed to hold oil and gas interests in Angola) held a 49% interest. The Angolan government was impressed enough to engage Executive Outcomes to help the army reclaim diamond fields in Angola's northeast. A DiamondWorks subsidiary then received a concession to commercialise diamond production from the government. The pattern repeated itself in Sierra Leone during that country's violent conflict, although DiamondWorks claimed there were no connections between government contracts with Executive

Outcomes to help secure diamond fields in 1996 and conces-
sions subsequently awarded to DiamondWorks.[2]

In between the Dutch East India Company of the seventeenth century and the DiamondWorks of the late twentieth, a
seemingly unbroken history of corporate violence shaped one
picture of the multinational corporation within the contemporary imagination: the profit-hungry, soulless and seemingly
stateless enterprise willing to exploit fragile conditions, strike
deals with unsavoury actors and foment conflict for economic
gain. In this narrative, predatory multinational companies
are a cause of conflict. Such stories therefore also provide the
logic for one contemporary international response to business
and conflict in fragile states: legal-regulatory approaches that
attempt to contain the worst forms of corporate conduct in the
face of those companies' political power.

The narrative of the predatory multinational company

The narrative of the predatory multinational company has
perhaps its deepest roots in the transatlantic slave trade, 'often
regarded as the first system of globalization'.[3] Although it was
launched by the Portuguese in the fifteenth century, it 'developed on an unprecedented scale when the major European
trading companies – Dutch, English and French in particular
– funded the expeditions as well as the exploitation of the
mineral and agricultural resources of the newly conquered
territories in the Americas'.[4] Of the 15–18 million people sold
as slaves in the western hemisphere:

> More than half of them were employed on the sugar
> cane plantations in the Caribbean and in Brazil, where
> their life expectancy did not exceed five to six years
> after their arrival. It was a deadly system in which it is
> estimated that for every African captive who reached

the Americas alive, five others died during the various phases of raiding, conflict and capture in the villages of the continental hinterland, during the forced march towards the assembly centres and trading posts, and during imprisonment in the baracoons on the African shores and subsequently during the transatlantic crossing.[5]

The Royal African Company (RAC), operating under a 1672 charter from King Charles II, quickly became the first among these transnational enterprises and accounted for more than half of all slave transports during the years of its operation. 'What a glorious and advantageous trade this is. It is the hinge on which all the trade of this globe moves', opined James Houstoun, a slave trader.[6] In addition to the heinous consequences of slavery itself, the RAC contributed to violence by exchanging 150,000 guns annually for African slaves.[7]

Multinational companies and imperial policy became deeply intertwined. Whereas conquest before this period was largely the business of government, European powers found that they could build and control empires more cheaply and effectively through innovative forms of public–private partnership. The Governor and Company of Adventurers of England trading into Hudson's Bay, later the Hudson's Bay Company, was emblematic of this approach. Its 1670 English royal charter made the company 'the true and absolute Lords and Proprietors' of the lands defined by the Hudson Bay watershed, representing roughly 40% of present-day Canada. The intention was unambiguously imperial: the land would be 'reckoned and reputed as one of our Plantations or Colonies in America'. To exercise its charter, the company could at will promulgate 'Laws, Constitutions, Orders, and Ordinances', impose 'Pains, Penalties and Punishments upon all Offenders', and perhaps more ominously, 'continue or make Peace or War with any Prince or People whatsoever' – as its corporate board deemed fit, and without government oversight.[8]

Sovereign power enabled companies to act with impunity for profit motives. The motto of Peter Skene Ogden, a chief trader of the Hudson's Bay Company, was that 'necessity has no laws'. As a clerk for the rival North West Company, he had been part of the growing violence between the two companies that eventually led the Crown to force their merger in 1821. According to the Hudson's Bay Company's own records, Ogden and his men 'butchered in a most cruel manner' an Indian who was trading with Hudson's Bay Company rather than North West Company. The Hudson's Bay Company's governor Joseph Berens, noting that Ogden's father was a judge, wrote to Lord Bathurst, secretary of state for war and the colonies, that Ogden 'cannot surely shelter himself under the plea of not knowing right from wrong or grounding thereupon an excuse for murdering an Indian in cold blood'.[9] Nevertheless, the Hudson's Bay Company in 1824 appointed Ogden as a chief trader tasked 'to destroy as fast as possible' the trapping grounds south of the Columbia River. By creating an environmental dead zone, it undermined American trade and settlement in the contested territory to protect the Company's interests. In his journal, Ogden noted denying American traders access to Company snowshoes to keep them from hunting, and ignoring pleas to assist the starving.[10] Ogden later went on to lead Company campaigns against the Russians on the Northwest Coast.

The use of private companies to create empires added a thread of political duplicity to the narrative of the predatory multinational company. Companies not only generated greater wealth at lower risk than could be achieved by direct conquest; they also provided political cover for European governments vis-à-vis their own constituents.

> [I]f a company's operation ran into any kind of trouble
> that would embarrass the government, the govern-
> ment could easily disown the company. Second,
> governments found it easier to circumvent opposi-
> tions to the colonial project by the use of the company
> ... [that] could take more drastic steps to achieve its
> aim than governments could.[11]

In its campaign against the Ndebele people to conquer what is now Zimbabwe, the British South Africa Company (BSAC) burned compounds and confiscated cattle, in one case using a cannon to kill 21 Africans in a retaliatory raid. Cecil Rhodes, who led the BSAC, wrote, 'I am glad to hear that you are maintaining the dignity of the law.'[12] Such acts did not go unnoticed in Europe; the British periodical *Truth* called Rhodes 'the head of a gang of shady financiers' who operated 'on the principle that "godless heathen" ought to be mowed down with Maxim guns if they happen to inhabit a country where there may be gold'.[13]

But 'with every fraud, every war and every expropriation, shareholders and politicians back home winked and benefited enormously'.[14] The South Africa Committee of Parliament convened in 1897 to investigate the Jameson Raid, a failed attempt by BSAC police to mount an English insurrection against the Afrikaner government in the Transvaal that was a catalyst for both the Second Boer War and the Second Matabele War. When the committee effectively took no action, Rhodes observed to Lord Grey, a BSAC director: 'There will be all sorts of surmises, conjectures, and suspicions for a week or so and then indifference and forgetfulness.'[15] Companies could expropriate land, exploit forced labour, or tear men from their families and communities to live in labour compounds around mines – despite the formal abolition of slavery by the home government over the course of the nineteenth century. But plausible deniability and lack of meaningful oversight of companies operating in faraway places allowed prominent stockholders as well as imperial proponents in European capitals to overlook such 'drastic steps' in the pursuit of wealth.

The negative view of the predatory multinational corporation took on a new dimension as governments found that private companies operated for their own benefit, rather than for that of the government that had chartered them. Jameson's raid to extend BSAC influence in the Transvaal had not only been an embarrassment, it had left the Rhodesian territory largely defenceless and created the opening for the 1896 Matabeleland Rebellion, its white settler, Ndebele and Shona deaths, and the destruction of farmsteads, fields and cattle. In North America, British officials over time found the Hudson's Bay Company much less cooperative in its aims against the French than it had anticipated. In the seventeenth century, the Hudson Bay was a theatre of war between the French and Hudson's Bay Company as a proxy for the Crown. By the eighteenth century, however – and despite 'the anti-French discourse that was typical of official HBC discourse' – the company remained 'effectively neutral', as conflict undermined the fur trade.[16] Coen's persistent campaign against the British in Indonesia flew in the face of an agreement between the two national governments to 'forgive and forget' past hostilities, return captured ships and prisoners, and 'henceforth live and converse as trusted friends'.[17]

These early multinational companies were seen not only as predatory towards the societies in which they operated, but they were increasingly understood as acting somewhere between a 'non-state realm', beside the likes of 'pirates and freelance soldiers' and 'imperial actors, *bona fide* states themselves'.[18] The picture of the multinational corporation emerged as answerable to no law or governmental authority, and loyal not even to the state that had created it.

Indeed, the multinational corporation came to be seen as a manipulator of the state system itself. In the US, strongly intertwined networks of political and commercial interests drove policy in Latin America. The Roosevelt Corollary to the Monroe Doctrine, introduced by President Roosevelt in his State of the Union address in 1904, stated in part that 'the United States would intervene as a last resort to ensure that other nations in the Western Hemisphere fulfilled their obligations to international creditors', justifying US intervention in Cuba, Nicaragua, Haiti and the Dominican Republic.[19] President Taft's 'Dollar Diplomacy', which held that 'the goal of diplomacy was to create stability and order abroad that would best promote American commercial interests', was developed by Secretary of State Philander C. Knox, a corporate attorney who had founded US Steel.[20]

Companies such as United Fruit could depend on these policies to guarantee their operations in fragile states such as Guatemala. A former United Fruit executive explained that 'Guatemala was chosen as the site for the company's earliest development activities because at the time we entered Central America, Guatemala's government was the region's weakest, most corrupt and most pliable'.[21] International Railways of Central America (IRCA), a United Fruit subsidiary, told its shareholders that they should welcome the ascent to power in 1931 of General Jorge Ubico, a dictator of note even in this volatile region.[22] Among other measures, he forbade the use of 'communist' expressions such as 'trade unions', 'strikes', 'labour rights' or 'petitions', and made it legal 'for the landowners to murder stubborn or rebellious Indians'.[23]

Labour market and other economic reforms after Ubico's ouster in 1944, however, culminated in the election in 1951 of

Jacobo Arbenz as president of Guatemala. He worked to break United Fruit's monopolies in transportation, shipping and electricity. He also began expropriations of United Fruit lands in 1953. Prompt payment was made, based on the land value United Fruit had previously declared in its tax filings.

When United Fruit's mobilisation of US diplomatic pressure to protect its interests did not have the intended effect, the Eisenhower administration agreed to overthrow Arbenz, supporting rebels who, upon taking power, rolled back Arbenz's reforms.[24] At the time, Eisenhower's secretary of state was John Foster Dulles who, as a law partner at Sullivan & Cromwell, had negotiated United Fruit's land deals with Ubico; Eisenhower's head of the CIA was Dulles's brother Allen, who had previously served on United Fruit's board of directors; his ambassador to the United Nations (UN) was Henry Cabot Lodge, a large shareholder in United Fruit; and his personal secretary was Ann Whitman, married to Ed Whitman, head of public relations for United Fruit.[25] Predatory multinational companies appeared not only to be beyond the control of their home states – they were increasingly seen to be controlling state institutions and policy.

The globalisation trend of the 1980s and 1990s saw the narrative of the predatory multinational company come full circle. As in the conflict between the North West Company and Hudson's Bay Company in Canada, or the war between the Dutch East India Company and its rival English East India Company, companies were again seen as complicit in significant violence in which any local authorities were subsidiary to company power and interests.

With the end of the Cold War, conflict zones became an important part of the global economy. Different types of actors emerged that linked these places to international arms, commodity and financial markets, and facilitated the conversion of illicit and criminal profits into legitimate sources of revenue. Armed conflict was no longer necessarily fought in order to achieve political goals; rather, the aim of fighting was to perpetuate conflict for economic profits.[26] This change in strategy emphasised the economic functions and self-financing nature of civil wars, or simply a situation in which civil wars became 'the continuation of economics by other means' or 'a way of creating an alternative system of profit, power and even protection'.[27]

Indeed, the entire civil war in Sierra Leone was described as 'something different, something newer and more insidious: … a struggle between two rival groups supported by businessmen intent on gaining control of mineral wealth'.[28] On the one side, De Beers and Lazare Kaplan International bought cheap diamonds from Charles Taylor in Liberia, 'responsible for aiding and abetting as well as planning some of the most heinous and brutal crimes recorded in human history', in the words of the Special Court for Sierra Leone.[29] He sourced the diamonds through the supply chain of the Revolutionary United Front rebels, whose operations across the border in Sierra Leone he supported. On the other side of the battle, companies such as Global Exploration Corporation, Rex Mining Corporation, DiamondWorks, and Sierra Rutile–Nord Resources directly or indirectly engaged mercenaries to claim control over the diamond fields that were exploited under agreements with President Ahmad Tejan Kabbah. The president's security forces were also responsible for gross human rights violations, including the use of child soldiers, the shelling of civilian positions, and the arbitrary executions of women and children as young as eight years old.[30] This was a violent conflict among multinational corporations in which one company would win handsomely, but the country itself would lose.

From the brutality of the Dutch East India Company in Indonesia in the early seventeenth century to twenty-first-century reports of violent and deathly reprisals against opponents of foreign mining and agribusiness interests in Guatemala, understood as the enduring sour fruits of neo-colonial, Cold War politics,[31] the narrative of the predatory multinational corporation at the root of violence emerged and crystallised over 400 years into one prominent contemporary understanding of business and conflict in fragile states.

Reining in the predatory company

If the unfettered predatory company is the cause of conflict and violence in fragile states, then its control is the solution. John Ruggie, special representative of the UN secretary-general on the issue of human rights and transnational corporations and other business enterprises from 2005–2011, linked the need for greater corporate regulation to the fragile states agenda when he noted that 'the worst cases of corporate-related human rights harm … occurred, predictably, where governance challenges were greatest: disproportionately in low-income countries; in countries that often had just emerged from or still were in conflict; and in countries where the rule of law was weak and levels of corruption high. A significant fraction of the allegations involved companies being complicit in the acts of governments or armed factions.'[32] His conclusion in 2008 was that 'governance gaps provide the permissive conditions for wrongful acts by companies of all kinds without adequate sanctioning or reparation. How to narrow and ultimately bridge the gaps in relation to human rights is our fundamental challenge.'[33]

Yet the roots of this focus on the regulation of the predatory company predate the contemporary discourse on business and human rights by some centuries, growing with organised opposition to the slave trade. The abolitionist movement in the UK grew in influence in the late eighteenth century. Tactically, this movement was organised in 1787 as the Society for Effecting the Abolition of the African Slave Trade, for it was thought that parliament would be more open to the suppression of what were characterised as evil enterprises than the institution of slavery itself.[34] A powerful West India Lobby ensured that the 1791 anti-slavery bill would be defeated by 163 votes to 88. But changes in public opinion as well as a more hospitable parliament – enabled by the entry of 100 Irish parliamentarians under the 1800 Act of Union – ensured passage of the 1807 Abolition of the Slave Trade Act by 283 votes to 16. In highlighting the barbaric practices of the slave traders, anti-slavery activists leveraged a generalised distrust of powerful corporations, captured in the pronouncement of Edward Thurlow, a Lord Chancellor of Great Britain in the late eighteenth century, that 'Corporations have neither bodies to be punished, nor souls to be condemned; they therefore do as they like.'[35]

Not only did the Abolition of the Slave Trade Act end the slave trade formalised by the charter granted to the Royal African Company in 1672 in Britain. Regulation of multinational enterprises briefly took on a transnational dimension when the Royal Navy was ordered to suppress slave traders, whether British or foreign. The Act provided that captains engaged in the trade could be fined £100 for each enslaved person on board – an enormous amount when considering that a skilled engineer would make about £110 in wages per year in this period.[36] Navy crews earned incentive pay tied to the number of slaves liberated and the tonnage of the ships seized and ultimately auctioned. 'Between 1807 and 1860, the Royal Navy, West Africa Squadron seized approximately 1,600 ships involved in the slave trade and freed 150,000 Africans who were aboard these vessels.'[37] Suppression of the slave trade, although itself embroiled in the expansion of empire in

West Africa, is noted as 'the first humanitarian rights issue that Britain pursued beyond its borders'.[38]

In the same era, imperial authorities also began to rein in the rights of the great chartered companies, in part because the companies' embroilment in conflict and violence was increasingly understood as being at odds with state interests. King Charles II in 1661 had expanded the already formidable powers of the East India Company to include 'the right to seize Interlopers, wage war and make peace with non-Christian princes, appoint governors, and exercise civil and criminal jurisdiction in its various settlements',[39] and in 1683 to 'confiscate the goods and ships of rivals'.[40] After the Company's mismanagement of the 1770 Bengal famine contributed to 10m dead and an economy in ruins, however, the Company came under increasing state control, beginning with the East India Company Act 1784.

When the Company used its powers to engage in illegal drug trafficking – a catalyst for the 1839 Opium War with China – William Ewart Gladstone (later prime minister) protested that it was an 'unjust and iniquitous' war 'to protect an infamous contraband traffic'.[41] In the wake of the Indian Rebellion of 1857, the Government of India Act of 1858 removed the last of the Company's sovereign powers, and it was dissolved with the East India Stock Dividend Redemption Act 1873. With the Company having been stripped of its power to make war, its monopolies, its administration of India, and eventually, its existence, the empire would grow, in the estimation of some, 'unfettered and unchecked by the restrictions, the cupidity, or the folly of an unworthy corporation'.[42]

From the perspective of those telling the story of the predatory multinational corporation, the challenge over the ensuing 150 years has been the rallying of sufficient political will for international action to contain corporate abuses. As illustrated by the demise of the chartered companies, the authority of a government to design and implement a legal regime to control its own corporations or those operating within its borders has never been in serious question. But in the context of fragile states, such regulation may not happen for a variety of reasons rooted in the political economy of both fragile states and companies' own home governments:

> First, the judiciary of the host state might be too weak to effectively control a powerful corporation. Where there is a weak or non-existing judiciary, the corporation might join forces with powerful domestic non-state actors exercising de facto control over the territory. Second, even if the host state has the necessary capacity, it might not wish to sanction the corporation as the host state might be corrupt or otherwise profit from or participate in the corporation's operations. Alternatively, in what is sometimes referred to as a 'race to the bottom', the state might want to retain an 'investor-friendly' environment with little public interference and lax regulation and enforcement in order to attract foreign investors. Third, sanctioning extraterritorial corporate behavior might be a low-priority task in the home state. The negative consequences of the activity are typically felt abroad, while the home state might benefit economically from the activity and even be facilitating it. Fourth, even if the home state wants to interfere, interference might be difficult because the activity takes place in another state. Regulating corporations is inherently complex for any state, regardless of the state's relative power, because of distance and because the home state may not enforce investigative or other measures. Sometimes *forum non conveniens*

findings prevent home states from seizing jurisdiction. Fifth, the home state might be reluctant to give its laws extraterritorial application due to the entailed risk of interstate friction.[43]

The question of business and conflict in fragile states over the past half century in particular became understood as the search for mechanisms to restrain the predatory multinational company in the absence of a willing or sufficiently capable national government in the country of operations, and relative indifference in the company's home country. This search took on greater urgency in the 1980s as ever more multinational companies extended their global reach, leveraging technology that fostered the integration of business, technological and financial systems which in turn stimulated a freer flow of capital, commodities and services across national borders.[44] Strategies include attempts to build the resolve to regulate transnational enterprises and punish wrongdoing in home state legal regimes; to create international interstate obligations for national governments to do so; to directly and indirectly control the flows of international capital that support multinational companies complicit in conflict and violence; and to create an international regime for civil and criminal liability for corporate misdeeds.

International non-profit organisations as well as interstate organisations in the first instance shed light on corporate complicity with conflict and violence in fragile states, working to motivate companies' domestic constituencies to action against the predatory company. Organisations such as non-governmental organisation (NGO) Global Witness focus on the nexus of corruption, violence and commercial interests. This may be in fragile states themselves, for example, Global Witness's 2001 exposé of the links between the military arm of the governing Zimbabwe African National Union–Patriotic Front and an enormous timber concession in the Democratic Republic of the Congo (DRC),[45] which was halted. Or alternatively it may be in home states, such as the organisation's 2003 investigation into money laundering by the Washington, DC Riggs Bank on behalf of Equatorial Guinea's president Teodoro Obiang, which contributed to the forced sale of the bank.[46] The UN Panel of Experts on the Illegal Exploitation of Natural Resources and Other Forms of Wealth of the DRC concluded that:

> A number of companies have been involved and have fuelled the war directly, trading arms for natural resources. Others have facilitated access to financial resources, which are used to purchase weapons. Companies trading minerals, which the Panel considered to be 'the engine of the conflict in the [DRC]', have prepared the field for illegal mining activities in the country.[47]

The Panel later named 85 corporations operating in violation of the Organisation for Economic Co-operation and Development (OECD)'s Guidelines for Multinational Enterprises.[48] The Panel had no direct regulatory powers. But as a result of the Panel's findings and subsequent debate, some companies stopped operations in the DRC, and others, though not all, made changes in their operating practices.[49]

Whether in response to such 'naming and shaming' campaigns or otherwise, states do on occasion rally political will to address through regulation the real or potential complicity of their companies in fragile state conflict and violence. A prominent contemporary expression is found in the requirements of Section 1502 ('Conflict Minerals Statutory Provision') of the

Dodd–Frank Wall Street Reform and Consumer Protection Act. These impose disclosure and due diligence obligations concerning conflict minerals that originate in the DRC or an adjoining country. They have their historical roots in the understanding of the role of 'blood diamonds' (diamonds sold to finance armed conflict) growing out of the civil wars in Sierra Leone and Angola, and the subsequent attention paid to 'conflict gold', 'conflict timber' and 'conflict minerals' elsewhere. The US Securities and Exchange Commission (SEC) understands 'Congress's main purpose to have been to attempt to inhibit the ability of armed groups ... to fund their activities by exploiting the trade in conflict minerals' through access to world markets via publicly traded companies that trade in, manufacture or have produced on their behalf products containing these minerals. In doing so, the SEC explains, Congress intended to address the humanitarian crisis, human rights abuses and threats to peace and security in the region.[50] As SEC regulations, they apply not only to enterprises formally incorporated or headquartered in the US, but to all companies listed on US stock exchanges. Yet such examples of home country regulation of company complicity in fragile state violence remain relatively rare.

A second avenue for home country regulation of the predatory company – by punishing its wrongdoing and presumably deterring further misdeeds – is pursued through private actions in the courts by victims of corporate abuses. These represent attempts to bypass the apparent resistance of governments and legislatures to look too closely at the role of their national companies in faraway conflicts. In the first case against a corporation under the US Alien Torts Claims Act, the Union Oil Company of California (Unocal) was at one stage of the proceedings found to have provided 'knowing practical assistance or encouragement that has a substantial effect on the perpetration' of crimes, in this case murder, torture, rape, and forced labour by the Myanmar army, which had been engaged by the company.[51] The company later settled with plaintiffs, reportedly for some tens of millions of dollars. Analogous cases have since been brought against companies accused of complicity in gross human rights violations in Argentina, Belgium, Canada, France, Germany, Japan, the Netherlands, South Korea, the UK and the US, sometimes resulting in substantial out-of-court settlements.

Yet the US Supreme Court's decision in 2013 to severely curtail the extraterritorial reach of the US courts[52] underlines that those hoping to hold companies to account in domestic legal forums encounter a system that is 'patchy, uneven, often ineffective and fragile ... In virtually every jurisdiction, victims of gross human rights abuses face significant obstacles to bringing a civil law claim against the corporate entities they hold responsible'.[53] How to 'ensure victims have access to judicial remedies in their States for abuses of human rights by transnational business', however, remains high on the agenda of advocates working to constrain and punish the predatory company.[54]

Acting on the assumption that collective approaches could lower political resistance to state action against corporate malfeasance in fragile environments, a variety of international initiatives to regulate corporate behaviour have worked to coordinate national responses and enshrine them in international and domestic law. As recently as 2000, for example, developed countries tacitly endorsed corruption by giving tax breaks to corporations for bribes they had paid abroad. OECD and UN treaties now require that state parties impose criminal sanctions for bribing a foreign public official,[55] with virtually all countries in the world signatories to one or both. The UN maintains more than a dozen sanctions lists pursuant to various Security Council resolutions that include corporate actors, each with its own measures that apply, the criteria for listing, and procedures for seeking delisting or exemptions to the measures.[56] These are not directly binding on companies, but rather are directives to UN member nations to take appropriate action vis-à-vis companies (and others) to limit travel, freeze assets or limit arms sales.

As demonstrated by faltering attempts to outlaw the use of mercenaries, however, states have proven reluctant to take action against corporate actors who may be seen under certain circumstances as useful. From the Biafra War in Nigeria (1967–1970) to the civil war in Angola (1975–2002), soldiers for hire became notorious for making already complex environments even more violent. In Papua New Guinea, the government of Prime Minister Julius Chan in 1996 engaged the services of Sandline International – another army for hire founded by (among others) Anthony Buckingham and sharing offices with his company Heritage Oil Ltd in London – to reclaim mining operations of one of the world's richest copper deposits in Bougainville, owned by a subsidiary of Rio Tinto. When the deal became public, it provoked a security crisis, the fall of the government and a lingering political crisis for the country. Sandline had proposed 'a joint venture ... to re-open and operate the Bougainville mine once recovered'.[57]

Even such examples did not generate the will among states to deal with the problem of the intertwined direct and indirect financial interests of mercenaries. Article 47 of the 1977 Additional Protocols of the Geneva Conventions made mercenaries subject to criminal prosecution by denying them combatant status.[58] The definition of a mercenary was so restrictive, however, that 'any mercenary who cannot exclude himself from this definition deserves to be shot – and his lawyer with him'.[59] The 1989 International Convention against the Recruitment, Use, Financing and Training of Mercenaries[60] has so far attracted only 33 state parties. As noted by the UN special rapporteur on the question of the use of mercenaries, this is at least in part because mercenaries in the contemporary period have become more often tools of governments than their enemies, even as they 'engage in activities which are apparently legal but are no less dangerous for the independence, economies, democracy and self-determination of the African peoples'.[61] In the home state, meanwhile, 'Sandline and its bedfellows, whether we like it or not, have become a tool with which Her Majesty's Government can implement aspects of its policy that are best kept at arms' length.'[62]

Partly in reaction to this state ambivalence towards the regulation of multinational companies – even those most directly implicated in fragile state violence – attention turned towards influence over private and public capital as a source of regulation of business. In the 1990s, Dutch newspapers publicised severe human rights abuses including torture, rape, physical intimidation and indiscriminate killing around the Grasberg mine in West Papua, Indonesia, operated by the American company Freeport-McMoRan through its Indonesian subsidiary PT Freeport. The company had supported the brutal force of the Indonesian army with funding and material support, including weapons and ammunition. Friends of the Earth (FOE), an international NGO with its secretariat in the Netherlands, had unsuccessfully attempted to sue Freeport in the US. It shifted its focus to ABN Amro (ABN) in the Netherlands, one of about 40 banks providing passive financing for the project. FOE garnered 800 signatures of ABN clients on a letter denouncing Freeport's behaviour, and convinced a number of Netherlands corporations to threaten to move their business. Management later recalled this campaign as a serious crisis for the bank.[63]

Such attention on the role of private capital in fragile state violence led to the creation of the Equator Principles in 2003, harmonised since 2012 with the International Finance Corporation (IFC) Performance Standards for identifying and managing environmental and social risk. These Standards require both the 80 financial institutions that have adhered to the Equator Principles and the IFC to verify as part of their environmental and social due diligence processes that recipients of bank financing comply with the IFC Performance Standards, to which they agree as a condition of any project finance loan. These Standards cover an exhaustive list of issues, among which are environmental and social risks and impacts; labour and working conditions; land acquisition and involuntary resettlement; and rights of indigenous peoples.[64]

While there is general complaint that the Standards are more honoured in their breach than in their observance,[65] they are contractually binding on a wide range of companies operating in fragile states; the IFC together with the Equator Principles banks issue 90% of all project finance loans globally.[66] The International Commission of Jurists (ICJ) has also suggested that the Standards open new avenues of redress for aggrieved parties in national courts. The ICJ notes that a company, pursuant to the Standards, makes contractually binding promises with the IFC or an Equator Principles bank, for example, to mitigate social or economic impacts; that a community may rely on these promises, for example, in giving its consent to a project; that the community may be hurt when the company fails to keep its promises; and that these factors, taken together, create a basis in most legal orders for the community, as a third-party beneficiary to the contract, to pursue damages against the company.[67]

Another form of regulation by international capital occurs when socially minded investors vote with their feet or engage in shareholder advocacy. CalPERS, the largest public pension fund in the US, has determined as a matter of policy that 'environmental, social, and corporate governance issues can affect the performance of investment portfolios', using these as a basis to filter investment decisions.[68] The Norwegian Government Pension Fund 'takes account of environmental, social and governance issues that could have a significant impact on the fund's value;'[69] may exclude companies from its portfolio on ethical grounds; and uses 'active ownership' to promote 'good business standards'.[70] The Fund's management is a visible player in international policy, votes at shareholder meetings and files shareholder proposals.

In the sphere of private capital, investors can be guided by conflict-sensitive independent investment research and advice, such as that from the UK-based EIRIS, which since 2013 incorporates the Conflict Risk Network, 'calling on corporate actors to fulfill their responsibility to respect human rights and to take steps that support peace and stability in areas affected by mass atrocities, genocide and other abuses'.[71] On the investment side, 'Investment in socially responsible mutual funds, exchanged-traded funds and similar vehicles soared almost 80% to over $1 trillion in 2012 from $569 billion in 2010 ... During the same two years, the number of social funds rose almost 50% to 740 from 493.'[72] Some asset management firms are taking an increasingly activist stance, for example becoming directly involved in negotiations over the adherence of portfolio companies to the Bangladesh Accord on Building and Fire Safety after the Rana Plaza factory collapse.[73]

Some existing international mechanisms do receive complaints involving corporate misconduct in fragile states. These include the World Bank's Inspection Panel set up in 1993,[74] and its Compliance Advisor Ombudsman (CAO) established in 1999 to address complaints involving the IFC or the Multilateral Investment Guarantee Agency (MIGA).[75] The International Labour Organization (ILO) may set up Commissions of Inquiry addressing obligations under ILO conventions,[76] and its Committee on Freedom of Association established in 1951 may consider specific complaints, of which there have been more than 3,000 in its history.[77]

Yet the CAO audit of IFC Investment in Corporación Dinant S.A. de C.V., Honduras, proves instructive in understanding the limitations of such mechanisms. The CAO audit found that the IFC's client Dinant had 'conducted, facilitated or supported forced evictions of farmers', that violence including multiple deaths 'occurred because of inappropriate use of private and public security forces under Dinant's control or influence', and that the 'IFC failed to identify early enough and/or respond appropriately to the situation of Dinant'.[78] The initial manage-ment response of the IFC, however, questioned the findings of the CAO audit; implied that most problems identified had already been addressed by changes in the IFC's Sustainability Framework; and highlighted positive company actions. Even after substantial protest against the IFC response led to revi-sions to the forward-looking action plan, there has been no mention of possible consequences for the company or avenues of redress for victims or their families for well-documented gross human rights abuses.[79] Designed primarily to determine whether the Bank is operating according to its own internal regulations, or to provide authoritative interpretations of ILO standards, respectively, neither World Bank nor ILO mecha-nisms can directly hold companies to account, restrain their activities, or punish their wrongdoing. And, as indicated in the Dinant case, they are substantially dependent on institutional goodwill for the implementation of their decisions.

Recognition that existing mechanisms are perhaps better at incremental, forward-looking improvement than at deterrence or punishment of wrongdoing has prompted activists to promote the establishment of an international tribunal that could hold the predatory multinational corporation to account. Such a mechanism has never existed in practice, even for gross abuses. Managers, directors and owners of German industrial concerns that exploited slave labour or were complicit in Nazi death camps were tried and convicted at Nuremberg for international crimes. Although 'corporate and associational criminal liability was seriously explored, and was never rejected as legally unsound', no action was brought against a company as such.[80] Neither did the Charters of the ad hoc tribunals for the former Yugoslavia and Rwanda, or that of the International Criminal Court, include corporations as possible defendants.[81]

Acknowledging frustration with these perceived gaps in international oversight of transnational malfeasance in fragile environments, the UN Human Rights Council in 2014 established an 'intergovernmental working group on transnational corporations and other business enterprises with respect to human rights; whose mandate shall be to elaborate an international legally binding instrument to regulate, in international human rights law, the activities of transnational corporations and other business enterprises'.[82] Other advocates (also in 2014) laid out a design for an International Arbitration Tribunal on Business and Human Rights to which companies could be compelled or encouraged to submit disputes.[83] Yet these initiatives remain largely aspirational.

Thus the legal-regulatory response to the narrative of the predatory multinational company remains full of ambiguity, as perhaps best illustrated by the UN Guiding Principles on Business and Human Rights – endorsed by the UN Human Rights Council in June 2011 to promote respect of human rights by business enterprises. On the one hand, even as their author posited that their 'normative contribution lies not in the creation of new international law obligations but in elaborating the implications of existing standards and practices for States and businesses',[84] the Guiding Principles represent the triumph of twin notions. First is the idea that companies must respect human rights, even in the weak rule-of-law and conflict-prone environments of fragile states (the 'Respect' pillar). Second is the premise that victims of corporate malfeasance, complicity or even neglect have the right to effective redress of their grievances (the 'Remedy' pillar).[85] These dual principles have in short order become central to national and international discourse. They have contributed to developments as diverse as revisions of corporations law in the European Union[86] and new legal defence strategies for developing countries when they are subject to arbitration actions by companies under bilateral investment treaties.[87] On the other hand, the Guiding Principles provide few if any answers to the question of how the predatory multinational company should be restrained or punished, other than to exhort states to do so (the 'Protect' pillar), garnering significant criticism from advocates.[88]

This ambiguity represented by the Guiding Principles plays itself out in multi-stakeholder initiatives such as the Voluntary Principles on Security and Human Rights (established in 2000), which addresses the complicity of extractives companies in violence by public or private security forces,[89] or the Kimberley Process Certification Scheme (created in 2002), which addresses the flow of conflict diamonds.[90] Certain civil society representatives and companies have acknowledged minimum standards of conduct for companies operating in, or trading with, fragile states. But even as advocates attempt to use such standards to hold multinational corporations to account, companies highlight their participation in voluntary processes. They do this both to distance themselves from the narrative of the predatory multinational company – claiming to be a different kind of company – and to maintain the essentially unenforced nature of the international regulatory regime – asserting that voluntary standards are sufficient.

Meanwhile, the Kimberley Process certified Zimbabwean diamonds as conflict free, despite widespread terror and violence in the diamond industry there.[91] The Kimberley Process's prohibition of 'rough diamonds used by rebel movements to finance wars against legitimate governments'[92] was found not to be relevant to the violence perpetrated by the Zimbabwean security forces against its own people; the Chair of the Kimberley Process went so far as to call on the US to lift its unilateral sanctions on diamonds from Zimbabwe, as the European Union had done.[93] Such stories reinforce for many the narrative of the predatory multinational company deeply enmeshed in fragile state conflict and violence, and capable of manipulating both host- and home-state governments to pursue its greedy ends.

Restraint of the predatory company as a goal of international policy

This chapter does not purport to provide a full treatment of the emergence of the narrative of the predatory multinational company since the Dutch East India Company provided a dramatic opening chapter in 1602. Rather, it illustrates that there has been an enduring narrative of corporate malfeasance at the root of one contemporary understanding of business and conflict in fragile environments. Recent headlines relating to alleged environmental indifference by Chevron in Ecuador, complicity in violence by British oil companies Shell in Nigeria and Soco International in Uganda, or failures of Dow/Union Carbide to confront the full impact of its Bhopal disaster in India show that the elements of this narrative that developed over centuries – corporate greed, indifference to suffering, willingness to use and promote violence, political and legal manipulation, loyalty to no master, and impunity – maintain strong contemporary currency.

Neither does this chapter represent a comprehensive survey of all the domestic and international initiatives to make illegal those corporate actions that foment conflict and violence in fragile environments, or to restrain and punish corporate misdeeds. Furthermore, while recognising certain well-documented cases of corporate complicity in fragile state conflict and violence, this chapter cannot assess the extent to which such behaviour is representative of multinational businesses in fragile environments.

Instead, this chapter more modestly shows that a common thread throughout the legal-regulatory approach to business and conflict in fragile states is the premise that international business itself causes instability and conflict around its operations. Overall, it highlights one key assumption underlying contemporary discourse: if businesses can be compelled to follow increasingly well-articulated and well-enforced rules and norms, then business-related violence can be contained, and conflict managed, in fragile states.

Notes

1. Stephen R. Bown, 'First Among Equals: Jan Pieterszoon Coen and the Dutch East India Company', in *Merchant Kings: When Companies Ruled the World, 1600–1900* (New York: Thomas Dunne Books, 2010), p. 46.

2. Madelaine Drohan, 'Ranger Oil in Angola', in *Making a Killing: How and Why Corporations Use Armed Force to Do Business* (Guilford: Lyons Press, 2004), chapter 7.

3. Katérina Stenou (ed.), *Struggles Against Slavery: International Year to Commemorate the Struggle Against Slavery and its Abolition* (Paris: UNESCO, 2004), p. 49.

4. *Ibid.*

5. *Ibid.*

6. James Houstoun, *Some New and Accurate Observations of Geographical, Natural and Historical. Containing a True and Impartial Account of the Situation, Product, and Natural History of the Coast of Guinea, So far as Relates to the Improvement of that Trade, for the Advantage of Great Britain in General, and the Royal Africa Company in Particular* (London: J. Peele, 1725), p. 44.

7   Fred W. Hackwood, *A History of Darlaston, Near Wednesbury* (Wednesbury: Woden Press, 1908).

8   *The Royal Charter for Incorporating the Hudson's Bay Company Granted by His Majesty King Charles the Second, in the Twenty-second Year of His Reign, A.D. 1670* (London: R. Causton & Son, 1816).

9   Glyndwr Williams, 'Ogden, Peter Skene', in *Dictionary of Canadian Biography*, vol. 8 (2003), http://www. biographi.ca/en/bio/ogden_peter_ skene_8E.html.

10 Barry M. Gough, 'The Hudson's Bay Company and the Imperialism of Monopoly: A Review Article', *BC Studies*, no. 18, summer 1973, pp. 70–8.

11 Olufemi Amao, *Corporate Social Responsibility, Human Rights and the Law: Multinational Corporations in Developing Countries* (New York: Routledge, 2011), p. 14.

12 Drohan, *Making a Killing: How and Why Corporations Use Armed Force to Do Business*, p. 26.

13 *Truth* (London), 30 November 1893.

14 Timothy Brook, 'Greed and Superprofits', *Toronto Globe and Mail*, 2 October 2009.

15 Robert I. Rotberg, *The Founder: Cecil Rhodes and the Pursuit of Power* (Oxford: Oxford University Press, 1990), p. 549.

16 Edward Cavanagh, 'A Company with Sovereignty and Subjects of its Own? The Case of the Hudson's Bay Company, 1670–1763', *Canadian Journal of Law and Society*, vol. 26, no. 1, 2011, p. 31.

17 Bown, *Merchant Kings*, p. 42.

18 Cavanagh, *A Company with Sovereignty and Subjects of its Own?*, p. 26.

19 Office of the Historian of the US Department of State, 'Roosevelt Corollary to the Monroe Doctrine', http://history. state.gov/milestones/1899-1913/ roosevelt-and-monroe-doctrine.

20 Office of the Historian of the US Department of State, 'Dollar Diplomacy 1909– 1913', http://history.state.gov/ milestones/1899-1913/dollar-diplo.

21 Peter Chapman, *Bananas: How the United Fruit Company Shaped the World* (New York: Canongate, 2008), p. 38.

22 IRCA, Annual Report 1931, p. 6.

23 Marcelo Bucheli, 'Good Dictator, Bad Dictator: United Fruit Company and Economic Nationalism in Central America in the Twentieth Century', University of Illinois at Urbana–Champaign, College of Business Working Paper (2006), p. 13.

24 *Ibid*.

25 Rich Cohen, *The Fish that Ate the Whale* (New York: Farrar, Straus and Giroux, 2012), p. 186.

26 Martin Van Creveld, *The Transformation of War* (New York: The Free Press, 1991), pp. 57–62.

27 David Keen, *The Economic Functions of Violence in Civil Wars*, Adelphi Paper No. 320, (London: IISS, 1998), p. 11.

28 Andrés Perez, 'Sierra Leone's Diamond Wars', *Le Monde Diplomatique* (English Edition), June 2000.

29 See Ben Brumfield, 'Charles Taylor Sentenced to 50 Years for War Crimes', CNN, 31 May 2012, http://edition.cnn. com/2012/05/30/world/africa/ netherlands-taylor-sentencing.

30 Truth and Reconciliation Commission, 'Sierra Leone, Witness to Truth: Report of the Sierra Leone Truth and Reconciliation Commission' (Accra: GPL Press, 2004).

31 Amnesty International, *Guatemala: Mining in Guatemala: Rights at Risk* (London: Amnesty International, 2014).

32 Office of the United Nations High Commissioner for Human Rights (OHCHR), 'Protect, Respect and Remedy: A Framework for Business and Human Rights', document no. A/HRC/8/5, 7 April 2008, p. 16.

33 *Ibid.*, p. 3.

34 Minutes of Committee for Abolition of Slavery, 22 May 1787, British Library, http://www.bl.uk/onlinegallery/takingliberties/staritems/66minutesofcommitteeabolition.html.

35 See John Poynder, *Literary Extracts*, vol. 1 (London: John Hatchard & Son, 1844), p. 268.

36 Clive Emsley, Tim Hitchcock and Robert Shoemaker, 'London History – Currency, Coinage and the Cost of Living', *Old Bailey Proceedings Online*, http://www.oldbaileyonline.org, version 7.0.

37 See 'Chasing Freedom: The Royal Navy and the Suppression of the Transatlantic Slave Trade', Royal Naval Museum, Portsmouth Historic Dockyard, http://www.history.ac.uk/1807commemorated/exhibitions/museums/chasing.html.

38 *Ibid.*

39 Marguerite Eyer Wilbur, *The East India Company and the British Empire in the Far East* (Brasted: Russell & Russell, 1970), p. 130.

40 *Ibid.*, p. 134.

41 Glenn Melancon, *Britain's China Policy and the Opium Crisis: Balancing Drugs, Violence and National Honour, 1833–1840* (Burlington: Ashgate, 2003), p. 126.

42 A contemporary press account, quoted in Arthur W. Silver, *Manchester Men and Indian Cotton* (Manchester: Manchester University Press, 1966), p. 109.

43 Ole Kristian Fauchald and Jo Stigen, 'Corporate Responsibility Before International Institutions', *George Washington International Law Review*, vol. 40, no. 4, 2009, pp. 1027–8.

44 Mark Duffield, 'Globalisation, Transborder Trade, and War Economies', in Mats Berdal and David M. Malone (eds), *Greed and Grievance: Economic Agendas in Civil Wars* (Boulder, CO: Lynne Rienner, 2000), pp. 69–70.

45 Global Witness, *Branching Out: Zimbabwe's Resource Colonialism in DRC* (London: Global Witness, 2001).

46 Paul Lashmar, 'The Bank that Liked to Say Yes to the Dirty Cash of Third World Dictators', *Independent*, 22 August 2004.

47 United Nations Security Council (UNSC), 'Report of the Panel of Experts on the Illegal Exploitation of Natural Resources and Other Forms of Wealth of the Democratic Republic of the Congo', document S/2001/357, para. 215.

48 UNSC, 'Final Report of the Panel of Experts on the Illegal Exploitation of Natural Resources and Other Forms of Wealth of the Democratic Republic of the Congo', document S/2002/1146, paras 170–8.

49 Rights and Accountability in Development (RAID), *Unanswered

Questions: Companies, Conflict and the Democratic Republic of Congo (Oxford: RAID, 2004).

50 Securities And Exchange Commission, 17 CFR PARTS 240 and 249b, effective 13 November 2012.

51 Doe I v. Unocal, 395 F.3d 932 (9th Cir. 2002).

52 Kiobel v. Royal Dutch Petroleum Co., 133 S.Ct. 1659 (2013).

53 Jennifer Zerk, 'Corporate Liability for Gross Human Rights Abuses: Towards a Fairer and More Effective System of Domestic Law Remedies', report prepared for OHCHR (2013), p. 103.

54 Gwynne Skinner, Robert McCorquodale and Olivier De Schutter, *The Third Pillar: Access to Judicial Remedies for Human Rights Violations by Transnational Business* (Washington DC: International Corporate Accountability Roundtable, 2013), p. 1.

55 Organisation for Economic Co-operation and Development Convention on Combating Bribery of Foreign Public Officials in International Business Transactions, 17 December 1998, 37 I.L.M. 1. United Nations Convention Against Corruption, 4 December 2000, 43 I.L.M. 37.

56 See Consolidated United Nations Security Council Sanctions List, http://www.un.org/sc/committees/list_compend.shtml.

57 Christopher Wrigley, *The Privatization of Violence: New Mercenaries and the State* (London: Campaign Against Arms Trade, 1999), https://www.caat.org.uk/resources/publications/government/mercenaries-1999.

58 Official commentary, 'Protocol Additional to the Geneva Conventions of 12 August 1949, and relating to the Protection of Victims of International Armed Conflicts (Protocol I)', 8 June 1977.

59 Geoffrey Best, c.f. David Shearer, *Private Armies and Military Intervention*, Adelphi Paper No. 316 (London: IISS, 1998), p. 18.

60 UNO Treaty Series, Volume 2163, 1–3 7789, entry into force 20 October 2001.

61 United Nations General Assembly (UNGA), *Report by Enrique Bernales Ballesteros, Special Rapporteur on the Question of the Use of Mercenaries*, document A/52/495 (New York: United Nations, 1997), para. 71.

62 See Wrigley, *The Privatization of Violence*.

63 Herman Mulder with Jonathan Martin, 'What Are We Accountable For? ABN Amro in Indonesia', in Brian Ganson (ed.), *Management in Complex Environments: Questions for Leaders* (Stockholm: International Council of Swedish Industry, 2013), pp. 103–5.

64 International Finance Corporation (IFC), *IFC Sustainability Framework: Policy and Performance Standards on Environmental and Social Sustainability* (Washington, DC: IFC, 2012).

65 See, e.g., Sasha Chavkin, Ben Hallman, Michael Hudson, Cécile Schilis-Gallego and Shane Shifflett, 'How the World Bank Broke its Promise to Protect the Poor', in *Evicted and Abandoned: The World Bank's Broken Promise to the Poor* (Washington, DC: International Consortium of Investigative Journalists, 16 April 2015), http://

www.icij.org/project/world-bank/how-world-bank-broke-its-promise-protect-poor.

66 IFC, 'IFC History', http://www.ifc.org/wps/wcm/connect/corp_ext_content/ifc_external_corporate_site/about+ifc/ifc+history#.

67 International Commission of Jurists (ICJ), *Report of the Expert Legal Panel on Corporate Complicity in International Crimes* (Geneva: ICJ, 2008).

68 CalPERS, Global Governance Principles (2015), p. 6.

69 Norges Bank, '2014 Responsible Investment Report: Government Pension Fund Global', 2015, p. 11.

70 *Ibid.*, p. 7.

71 See EIRIS Conflict Risk Network, http://www.eiris.org/about-us/eiris-conflict-risk-network.

72 Barry Rehfeld, 'Socially Responsible Funds Are Hot, But Are They Really Doing Good?', *The Street*, 6 November 2014.

73 Geeta Aiyer, 'Global Investment Community Can't Afford to Ignore Sustainability', *Guardian*, 14 November 2014.

74 International Bank for Reconstruction and Development (IBRD), 'The World Bank Inspection Panel', Resolution no. IBRD 93–10, 22 September 1993.

75 Office of the Compliance Advisor/Ombudsman (CAO) Terms of Reference (1999) as endorsed by the President of the World Bank Group, http://www.cao-ombudsman.org/about/whoweare/documents/TOR_CAO.pdf.

76 International Labour Organization (ILO) Constitution, articles 26–9, http://www.ilo.org/ilo lex/english/iloconst.htm.

77 ILO, *The Committee on Freedom of Association*, see http://www.ilo.org/global/standards/applying-and-promoting-international-labour-standards/committee-on-freedom-of-association/lang--en/index.htm.

78 CAO, 'CAO Audit of IFC Investment in Corporación Dinant S.A. de C.V., Honduras', CAO Audit Report C-I-R9-Y12-F161 (Washington DC: World Bank Group, 2013).

79 IFC Management Responses to CAO Audit, letters of January to October 2014, http://www.ifc.org/wps/wcm/connect/region__ext_content/regions/latin%20america%20and%20the%20caribbean/strategy/corporacion_dinant#mgmtresponse.

80 Jonathan A. Bush, 'The Prehistory of Corporations and Conspiracy in International Criminal Law: What Nuremberg Really Said', *Columbia Law Review*, vol. 109, no. 5, 2009, p. 1239.

81 *Ibid.*

82 Human Rights Council (HRC), 'Elaboration of an International Legally Binding Instrument on Transnational Corporations and Other Business Enterprises with Respect to Human Rights', document A/HRC/RES/26/9, 14 July 2014.

83 Claes Cronstedt, Robert C. Thompson, Rachel Chambers, Adrienne Margolis, David Rönnegard and Katherine Tyler, 'An International Arbitration Tribunal on Business and Human Rights: Reshaping the Judiciary', Version 3, 23 June 2014, http://business-humanrights.org/sites/default/files/media/documents/intl_arbitration_tribunal_version_3-23_june_2014.pdf.

84 John G. Ruggie, Presentation of Report to United Nations Human Rights Council, Geneva, 30 May 2011, p. 2, http://business-humanrights.org/sites/default/files/media/documents/ruggie-statement-to-un-human-rights-council-30-may-2011.pdf.

85 HRC, 'Guiding Principles on Business and Human Rights: Implementing the United Nations "Protect, Respect and Remedy" Framework', document A/HRC/17/31 (Geneva: United Nations, 2011).

86 Radu Mares, 'Business and Human Rights after Ruggie: Foundations, the Art of Simplification and the Imperative of Cumulative Progress', in Radu Mares (ed.), *The UN Guiding Principles on Business and Human Rights: Foundations and Implementation* (Leiden: Martinus Nijhoff, 2012), pp. 1–50.

87 Yousuf Aftab, 'The Intersection of Law and Corporate Social Responsibility: Human Rights Strategy and Litigation Readiness for Extractive-Sector Companies', 2014, http://business-humanrights. org/sites/default/files/documents/ YAftab-Rocky%20Mountain%20 Final%20%282014%29.pdf.

88 Jens Martens and Elisabeth Strohscheidt, *Problematic Pragmatism: The Ruggie Report 2008 – Background, Analysis and Perspectives* (Aachen and Bonn: MISEREOR and Global Policy Forum Europe, 2008).

89 Voluntary Principles on Security and Human Rights (2000), http://www.voluntaryprinciples.org/ wp-content/uploads/2013/03/ voluntary_principles_english.pdf.

90 Kimberley Process Certification Scheme (2002), http://www. kimberleyprocess.com/en/ kpcs-core-document.

91 Global Witness, *Financing a Parallel Government? The Involvement of the Secret Police and Military in Zimbabwe's Diamond, Cotton and Property Sectors* (London: Global Witness, 2012).

92 See Kimberley Process, http://www. kimberleyprocess.com.

93 NSNBC, 'Kimberley Process Demands Stop of US Ban on Zimbabwe Diamonds', NSNBC, 20 November 2013.

CHAPTER TWO

Business and peaceful development in fragile states

The Chamber of Mines in the Union of South Africa supported the Natives Land Act of 1913, which introduced territorial segregation to the country shortly after its founding in 1910. Reserves for the black population were created that represented only about 10% of the country's land area.[1] The president of the Chamber was of the opinion that the Act would ensure that 'the surplus of young men, instead of squatting on the land in idleness ... must earn their living by working for a wage'.[2] This guaranteed the mines cheap labour. The Chamber also supported the state's brutal suppression of successive waves of the black labour movement in the 1910s, the 1940s and the 1960s. Yet in the 1970s, the evident ability of labour to mount effective strikes, the need for more highly skilled workers, and the closing of labour recruitment from Malawi, Angola and Mozambique changed the mining landscape. By 1972 W.D. Wilson, Deputy Chairman of the mining conglomerate Anglo American Corporation, called for a 'major overhaul' of labour law and labour relations, stating that reforms would determine 'whether we will retain industrial peace and whether we will have the human resources to continue the development and expansion of our enterprises'.[3] Harry Oppenheimer, Chairman of Anglo American, declared that 'racial discrimination and free enterprise are basically incompatible'.[4] After the Soweto uprising of 1976, Oppenheimer and other leading industrialists founded the Urban Foundation to help improve the living conditions of the black urban population. Its first executive director stated that 'No free enterprise system can survive in circumstances of persistent social disruption and disorder.'[5]

Business engagement based on these changed notions was meaningful. Support for the Wiehahn Commission on labour reform and subsequent changes to the Industrial Conciliation Act led to the legalisation of black unions in 1979. Industry leaders, recognising that state agents could not be trusted by black employees, negotiated with labour leaders the creation of the Independent Mediation Service of South Africa (IMSSA) in 1984. In the same period in which the apartheid state increasingly used arrest, banning and assassination to stem the growing power of the unions, even bombing the headquarters of the Congress of South Africa Trade Unions in 1987, IMSSA constituted a regime of private justice acceptable to workers and companies. By 1990 IMSSA was mediating 580 workplace cases and arbitrating another 344 annually. Its legitimacy was such that it was able to act effectively outside the labour-management sphere. For example, the peace conference IMSSA organised in 1991 in Thokoza, a township near Johannesburg, 'led to a total cessation of politically related deaths for six months in a community in which 300 people had died in political violence in only 18 months'.[6]

At the national level, the Consultative Business Movement (CBM) was launched in 1988 to work with democratic forces inside the country and the African National Congress (ANC) in exile. In 1990 it organised a meeting of 40 ANC representatives, including Nelson Mandela, with 350 senior business leaders to reduce mutual distrust and start work towards a new national economic framework. When political violence put the entire peaceful transition to democracy in doubt, the CBM's relationships and credibility were such that it, along with the South African Council of Churches, was able to convene government and opposition parties in the offices of Barlow Rand Ltd, South Africa's second largest industrial concern. Its chairman and CEO, Mike Rosholt, had negotiated the first exemption from the apartheid law prohibiting more than 3% of black employees from being housed with their families on any mine, which forced nearly all black miners to live apart from their families for most of the year.[7]

The CBM-convened process was the beginning of negotiations leading up to the National Peace Accord in 1991. This in turn set the stage for constitutional negotiations. The CBM was asked by the participating political parties and government authorities to provide process support and secretariat services for the Convention for a Democratic South Africa (CODESA) I & II, two rounds of multi-party talks. The CBM later acted as the administration of the Multi-Party Negotiating Process, which put into motion South Africa's ultimate transition to democracy. And where Lord Carrington and Henry Kissinger had failed to secure the agreement of the Inkatha Freedom Party to participate in the first elections, risking renewed violence, the CBM-supported process succeeded. The CBM and Urban Foundation merged in 1995 to form the National Business Initiative, with a mission to continue private-sector engagement in South Africa's peaceful development.[8]

Such stories shape another picture of the multinational corporation as captured in contemporary discourse: the company working towards greater stability in fragile states out of enlightened self-interest. In this narrative, the private sector contributes to peaceful development directly through higher wages, greater respect for labour rights, the opening of new economic sectors or support for conflict resolution mechanisms, as well as indirectly by using their influence as powerful economic actors to curb the worst excesses of a corrupt state or encourage it to more progressive action. These examples therefore also provide the logic for the other dominant contemporary international response to business and conflict in fragile states: attempts to create an attractive environment for a vigorous private sector through liberal state-building, and increasingly, the enabling of ever more business influence in social, economic and political development.

Business as a foundation for peaceful development

The narrative of a robust private sector as a foundation for peaceful development has its roots in classical liberal outlooks on institutions and the economy. As early as 1689, the political philosopher John Locke argued that expanding entrepreneurship and property rights would lead to more peaceful government.[9] By 1884, the political economist John Stuart Mill claimed that 'it is commerce which is rapidly rendering war obsolete, by strengthening and multiplying the personal interests which are in natural opposition to it'.[10] Wharton Business School professor Howard V. Perlmutter, writing during the great post-war expansion of the multinational enterprise in the 1960s, echoed this thinking. He named 'the senior executives engaged in building the geocentric enterprise ... the most important social architects of the last third of the twentieth century. For the institution they are trying to erect promises a greater universal sharing of wealth and a consequent control of the explosive centrifugal tendencies of our evolving world community.' According to Perlmutter, this new geocentric enterprise offered 'an institutional and supra-national framework which could conceivably make war less likely, on the assumption that bombing customers, suppliers and employees is in nobody's interest'.[11] This classical view held that business interests would contain the destructive forces of conflict and war.

The contemporary reincarnation of such liberal thinking is more nuanced in light of the slave trade that flourished on the heels of Locke's argument, the century or more of European armed conflict that followed Mill's and the decades of turmoil that followed Perlmutter's. The premise is that a liberal economy – including factors such as the ease of establishing a business and widespread legal protections – 'significantly decreases the probability that a country will experience a dispute'.[12] Naked commerce or the mere presence of global enterprise might not be enough. But 'The flowering of economic freedom', argue political scientist Erik Gartzke and others, 'has begun to dampen the fires of war'.[13] Drawing on substantial macroeconomic and qualitative research, this worldview was summarised in Thomas Friedman's Golden Arches Theory of Conflict Prevention – 'No two countries that both had McDonald's had fought a war against each other since each got its McDonald's'[14] – later updated to the Dell Theory of Conflict Prevention – 'No two countries that are both part of a major global supply chain, like Dell's, will ever fight a war against each other as long as they are both part of the same global supply chain'.[15]

Despite evidence that commerce is not a panacea against conflict – Ukraine and Russia went to war despite their respective McDonald's, for example, and Russia remained Ukraine's largest trading partner through 2015, even at war – this enduring belief in liberal peace provides the predominant framework for international policy and institutions that seek to integrate the global economy and promote private enterprise to reduce conflict. Western policymakers perceive that 'empirical confirmation of the liberal peace is exceptionally strong', pointing to research findings that liberal democracies do not seem to fight wars against other liberal democracies.[16] Policymakers therefore pursue 'pacification through political and economic liberalization'[17] that will presumably expand the circle of nations at peace with each other.

The Bretton Woods institutions – the International Monetary Fund (IMF) and the International Bank for Reconstruction and Development (IBRD) – played leading roles in the post-war conversion of this ideology of business and peace into a series of four policy goals, the first of which was the policy of enabling national and international ecosystems in which private enterprise could flourish. The IMF was founded in the ashes of the Second World War 'to facilitate the expansion and balanced growth of international trade, and to contribute thereby to the promotion and maintenance of high levels of employment and real income and to the development of the productive resources of all members'.[18] 'It was understood,' said a former managing director of the IMF, 'that with stability would come peace and security.'[19] The IBRD was explicitly founded on a positive notion of business and conflict in fragile states, its first purpose being 'to assist in the reconstruction and development of territories of members … including the restoration of economies destroyed or disrupted by war' and its second 'to promote private foreign investment'.[20] In 1960 the International Development Association (IDA, together with IBRD 'the World Bank') extended the Bank's vision of the 'maintenance of peace and world prosperity' to the poorest nations, with lending on concessionary terms.[21]

The blueprint for policy reforms that evolved came to be known as the 'Washington Consensus', a term coined by economist John Williamson in 1990. While the exact contours of this blueprint remain contested, it is strongly associated with an international focus on macroeconomic stabilisation, trade liberalisation, the opening of domestic markets to foreign direct investment and the privatisation of state enterprises.[22] These steps were seen as crucial to a country's transition from poverty and instability to peace and development.

The direct support of private investors emerged as a second international policy goal. The Bretton Woods agreements had not originally anticipated private-sector finance as part of the new World Bank's stabilisation and development mission. But with the arrival of Robert L. Garner, a New York banker and later Financial Vice President and Director of the General Foods Corporation, such financing increasingly became central to the Bank's remit. He recalled, 'It was my firm conviction that the most promising future for the less developed countries was the establishing of good private industry.'[23]

The International Finance Corporation (IFC) was created in 1956 to make private-sector loans; this was expanded to private-sector investments in 1961, and in 1971 to the development of capital markets. By 1984 the IFC became financially independent of the World Bank, issuing its own bonds on world capital markets. It had effectively become a commercial bank, as underlined by its first AAA credit rating in 1989, while still articulating the goals to end extreme poverty and boost shared prosperity in developing countries.[24] As the Washington Consensus took root, regional and national institutions increasingly followed the IFC's lead. The African Development Bank, for example, founded in 1964, expanded its remit to private-sector development in October 1989 with its first Private Sector Development Strategy and Policy,[25] as did the Inter-American Development Bank in 1990.

This private-sector promotion by international financial institutions met the dual objective of opening up space for the private sector while closing space for the public sector.

For some, this was directly tied to addressing root causes of conflict. If the perception was that 'the new economic policy that emerged in African states after independence and transformed governments to rent-allocating agents (with powers as producers, allocators, and distributors of the social product) added to the sequence of maldevelopment', then 'the most obvious answer is market reform and liberalisation so as to attack the rent-seeking society'.[26]

The IFC's strategy now includes explicit focus on conflict-prone environments. Noting that 'nearly a quarter of the people on the planet live in areas torn by conflict and violence', the IFC in fiscal year 2015 invested more than US$600 million in fragile and conflict-affected regions, including syndicated loans.[27] Projects targeted towards post-conflict countries in earlier years included an IFC guarantee through its Global Trade Finance Program that enabled Morris American Rubber Company (MARCO) in Liberia to import rubber-processing machinery from Malaysia. The claim is that the company, which employs some 400 predominantly ex-combatant workers, is a growing part of a private sector that is the 'key driver' of job creation, economic growth and stability.[28] The IFC's Conflict Affected States in Africa (CASA) initiative for its part recognises the specific challenges of conflict-affected states, having been launched to provide 'tailored economic assistance specific to their needs'. Despite the IFC's claim of a distinctive response for conflict-prone states, however, the cocktail prescribed – 'reform the investment climate, strengthen financial markets, improve access to finance, and increase private sector participation in the provision of infrastructure'[29] – may seem hard to distinguish from the generic precepts of liberal peace.

In the tumultuous decades of decolonisation and anti-imperialism following the Second World War, a third focus of international policymakers became the protection of private investment. The first bilateral investment treaty (BIT) was entered into between Germany and Pakistan in 1959; the number of BITs has now grown to some 2,300 in force among more than 180 countries, as well as hundreds of other bilateral, regional and multilateral trade agreements with investment protection provisions.[30] These were understood from the beginning as an 'institutional means of protecting the private foreign investments of Western capital-exporting nations'[31] in even the most fragile states. While there are few binding international accords addressing even the most problematic company actions, systems of international arbitration allow companies' claims against developing country governments to be adjudicated and enforced under a BIT, an investment contract between the investor and the host state, or another investment protection regime. While the system formally applies equally to developed and developing countries, only 7% of the cases addressed by the World Bank's International Centre for the Settlement of Investment Disputes (ICSID) over the past decade involved a North American or Western European government as the state party, or party against which a claim was brought (while 68% of the arbitrators, conciliators and ad hoc committee members appointed by ICSID came from those regions).[32]

The World Bank Group further reinforced the connection of investor protection to the fragile states agenda with the creation of the Multilateral Investment Guarantee Agency (MIGA) in 1988. Its mission is 'to promote foreign direct investment by facilitating development projects in economies that do not attract foreign capital easily – countries in sub-Saharan Africa, post-conflict states, and the world's poorest states',[33] primarily by providing to investors insurance against political risks such as currency inconvertibility, expropriation, terrorism, or breach of contract by governments.

Such is the presumed importance of multinational businesses that foreign investors are typically accorded more rights in the developing country than they would be at home. Under domestic law, for example, a shareholder cannot typically bring a claim based on a so-called 'reflective loss incurred as a result of injury to "their" company (such as loss in value of shares)'. Only the company itself can make the claim. 'In contrast, shareholder claims for reflective loss have consistently been permitted under typical bilateral investment treaties (BITs) in recent years.'[34]

Furthermore, virtually any public policy of the host country can be challenged through the dispute settlement mechanism as long as it affects foreign investors. One oft-cited example is that of the US Renco Group, which is reported to have used the investor-state dispute settlement process in 1997 to pressure the government of Peru to allow it to reopen its subsidiary's smelter in La Oroya without installing legally mandated pollution-capturing devices.[35] The Blacksmith Institute later found the community to be one of the ten most polluted places in the world, noting lead levels in children's blood three times the World Health Organization limit.[36] The complaint by those suspicious of the international investment regime is that investor protections 'seriously restrict the ability of host states to regulate foreign investment',[37] requiring countries to 'trad[e] sovereignty for credibility'.[38] But in the narrative of business as a foundation for peaceful development, underlying demands for such investor protections is the supposition that it is the multinational company that legitimately fears the fragile state, not the other way around.

Elliot Berg's influential 1981 report, 'Accelerated Development in Sub-Saharan Africa: A Plan for Action',[39] provided a focal point for international policy on the reach and quality of fragile state governments, a fourth and enduring emphasis of international policy. In his 1998 work *Good Governance and Economic Development*, Karl Wohlmuth characterises the variety of approaches that multilateral and bilateral donors subsequently took to condition aid on the good governance agenda, particularly as it related to greater private sector development.[40] These include the 'state reform perspective' of the World Bank, focusing on the reform of policies and practices that discourage investment and, in the fragile states context specifically, the appropriation of government to serve elite interests. Under the notion of the effective state laid out in the 1997 *World Development Report* on the changing role of the state, investment (and therefore peace and development) will follow from getting the fundamentals of governance right. The IMF focused primarily on macroeconomic stability, geared towards the 'development and maintenance of a transparent and stable economic and regulatory environment that is conducive to efficient private sector activities'.[41] The United Nations Development Programme (UNDP), acting as a closer partner to governments – rather than through the aid conditionality that characterised the World Bank and IMF as well as many bilateral donor strategies – approached good governance through training programmes for public officials. The good governance agenda became further connected to the fragile state agenda as the United Nations Conference on Trade and Development (UNCTAD) and the United Nations Children's Fund (UNICEF), along with non-governmental organisations (NGOs) and Scandinavian donors in particular, focused on governance reform to prevent state collapse in light of the 'increasing number of countries with internal conflicts, border conflicts, and natural disasters'.[42] According to this policy intervention, 'Regressed economies and societies need a form of assistance that is directly related to rebuilding social, economic and state institutions.'[43] In the words of the

African Development Bank, 'Building legitimate and capable political and justice institutions, as well as resilient economic institutions, is at the heart of overcoming fragility and building resilient states.'[44]

Criticism of the narrative of free markets and a vigorous private sector as the centrepiece of peaceful development led to even greater emphasis on the importance of government institutions. 'The intellectual foundations of the Washington Consensus had been badly eroded even before its doctrines became widely accepted,' noted Joseph Stiglitz, former chief economist of the World Bank.[45] As it became recognised that 'countries that followed the Washington Consensus policies grew more slowly than those that did not' – contrasting, for example, anaemic results in IMF-dominated processes in Africa and Latin America with those of India and China – there was a growing sense that 'the objectives of development reflected in the Washington Consensus were too narrowly defined'.[46] These objectives were increasingly seen to prioritise GDP growth to the detriment of increases in standards of living and democratic and equitable development. Even those at the heart of the Washington Consensus invited greater attention to 'the institutional dimensions [and] the sort of policies… that promote an equitable distribution of income as well as a rapid growth of income'.[47] Others argued that there had been confusion of means and ends: privatisation and liberalisation had become the goals, rather than tools for achieving peaceful development in a particular context. 'An important role for government' became increasing widely accepted as it became apparent that there was no credible evidence that 'in early stages of development, markets by themselves will lead to efficient outcomes'.[48]

This led to an even sharper focus on the government institutional reform which had already become 'the main new thrust of development economics in the 15 years since the Washington Consensus was first promulgated'.[49] In the mid-1990s, many development agencies recognised that the effect of aid on economic growth and poverty reduction was greater in countries with 'good' policies and institutions.[50] Japan's state-led development approach, and the restructuring of the economies of Eastern Europe, also emphasised that the state can be an important development catalyst.[51] By the time the World Bank launched its Low-Income Countries Under Stress (LICUS) initiative in 2002, it was adopting 'state building as a central objective',[52] tied to private-sector development. This language is echoed in the Organisation for Economic Co-operation and Development (OECD) report 'Monitoring the Principles for Good International Engagement in Fragile States and Situations' (2007), which also calls for a 'focus on statebuilding as the central objective'.[53]

The doctrine of state-building remains the central pillar of the contemporary liberal narrative of business and conflict in fragile states. Robert B. Zoellick, at the time president of the World Bank Group, stated flatly in the foreword to the *World Development Report 2011: Conflict, Security and Development* that 'institutional legitimacy is the key to stability. When state institutions do not adequately protect citizens, guard against corruption, or provide access to justice; when markets do not provide job opportunities; or when communities have lost social cohesion – the likelihood of violent conflict increases.'[54] In the wake of the report, the Bank's IDA declared a new focus on 'strengthening legitimate institutions and governance to provide citizen security, justice and jobs' in fragile and conflict-affected states.[55]

One institutional manifestation was the Bank's establishment in 2011 of the Global Center for Conflict, Security and Development (CCSD) in Nairobi. Before this, in 2010, the African Legal Support Facility, hosted by the African Development Bank, had been established to increase the capacity of African governments 'to negotiate and conclude fair and equitable arrangements for the management of Africa's natural resources and extractive industries'.[56] More recently, the World Bank and the United Nations Environment Programme (UNEP) joined efforts to work with conflict-affected and fragile states to consolidate all existing information on resource concession, infrastructure, land use and risk information into a single open-source platform.[57] The 2013 Report of the High-Level Panel of Eminent Persons on the Post-2015 Development Agenda, commissioned by the UN Secretary-General, continues to call for more attention to 'effective, open and accountable institutions for all'.[58] As noted by Harvard professor Dani Rodrik, 'market fundamentalism' had become 'institutions fundamentalism'.[59]

A focus on government capacity- and institution-building has become the default international policy response to business and conflict, permeating most multilateral engagement with fragile state governments. Such thinking plays out in places like Uganda which, despite stable macro-economic policies and steady GDP growth, ranked as the world's 23rd-most fragile state on the 2015 Fragile States Index.[60] The central question for international policymakers became how to help the government develop its Albertine Graben oil reserves in ways that achieved the espoused goals of its 2008 National Oil and Gas Policy (itself formulated with international assistance), specifically that oil 'contribute to early achievement of poverty eradication and create lasting value to society', despite challenging socio-political conditions. It was recognised that Uganda in 2012 ranked 161st on the UN's Human Development Index and 143rd on Transparency International's Corruption Perceptions Index, and that the country was trending negatively on rule of law and accountability, human rights, and sustainable economic opportunity on the 2012 Ibrahim Index of African Governance.[61]

The answer to private sector development amidst fragility would be a stronger state. The UNDP, bilateral donors, international financial institutions and international development organisations funded and provided technical support for the development in Uganda of regulations, institutions, and accountability measures that espoused liberal values and developmental purposes. The 2012 Petroleum (Exploration, Development & Production) Bill stated its goals as 'creating a conducive environment for the efficient management of petroleum resources of Uganda'; 'establishing institutions to manage the petroleum resources and regulate the petroleum activities'; and 'providing for the optimal social and economic benefits of petroleum resources with a long term perspective for Ugandan society as a whole'. The Public Finance Bill declared 'a legal and regulatory framework for the collection, allocation and management of petroleum revenue in a responsible, transparent and accountable manner'. The non-partisan Parliamentary Forum on Oil and Gas, as well as the Civil Society Coalition for Oil in Uganda and its members – also supported by foreign donors and experts – worked to improve recognition of their role in 'advocacy, mobilization and dialogue with communities', as set out in the National Oil and Gas Policy.

Taken together, the foreign-supported model being implemented to govern oil development and the distribution of its hoped-for benefits in Uganda was one of strong state structures held accountable by parliamentary oversight and an engaged civil society.[62] In Chapter Four we look more closely at the impact of such efforts, including unintentional perverse impacts on conflict and violence; here, we only observe that the liberal narrative leads liberal institutions to be bolted on to the fragile state to manage business and conflict through a strong national government.

The narrative of a strong private sector as a foundation for peaceful development has remained relatively consistent from Locke and Mill to contemporary Uganda. It takes as axiomatic, as asserts the Freedom of Investment process – an intergovernmental forum on investment policy hosted since 2006 by the OECD Investment Committee – that 'international investment spurs prosperity and economic development'.[63] From this perspective, any failure of investment and economic growth to translate into conflict reduction and shared prosperity must be attributable to 'a country's politics. Political leaders may fight for power not to serve the country, but to get their hands on the resource revenues, which they can then use to buy votes and stay in power. In extreme cases, the availability of rents can lead to violent conflict over how they are spent.'[64] State-building efforts are therefore meant to help national governments better manage the questions of land, resource management and benefit sharing at the heart of conflicts over large-scale investments through better policy and regulation, institutions, and human capacity within the government.[65] Since in the liberal narrative the private sector is at the core of peaceful development, then weak national policy and institutions are seen as the root problem of business and conflict, and become the dominant focus of intervention.

Business as an agent for peaceful development

Tetra Pak, part of the Tetra Laval Group of companies focused on technologies for the production, packaging and distribution of food, works with a Bangladeshi milk-processing customer as well as with international NGOs and donors to establish dairy hubs. The manager of the commercial dairy hub is responsible for all aspects of the supply chain within the hub's geographic footprint. The hub provides free education to small-scale dairy farmers, and veterinary services at cost that ensure healthy cows, making available services that the country's agricultural ministry did not deliver. The hub collects and tests milk twice daily, guarantees the purchase of all quality milk produced and pays farmers weekly in cash, removing the problem of corrupt middlemen. It also collects data across its activities and can provide a comprehensive picture of the dairy value chain on a weekly basis. There is a single point of accountability, whether for the adequacy of milk production, the quality of vaccines, or processing and packaging efficiency.

The first hub opened in September 2010 in an area in which 30,000 litres of milk per month were available for purchase; that hub is now processing more than 500,000 litres per month. Where, before the establishment of the dairy hub, a family might have had one or two cows, it is now not uncommon for a family to have ten. More than 1,000 small-scale farmers moved from producing milk for family consumption or episodic sales to milk production as a primary source of family income. Farmers are paid more per litre of milk than they were before the establishment of the hubs, even while the processer's cost of acquisition per litre of milk has decreased and the quality of milk collected has increased.[66] These successes occurred in a country ranked by the Fragile States Index in 2015 as the 32nd-most fragile state in the world.[67] They also occurred despite the country's problem of corruption – Bangladesh ranked 145th out of 175 countries on Transparency International's 2014 Corruption Perceptions Index[68] – which undermines the ability of government-supported cooperatives to achieve similar positive results.

The lesson of such stories in the narrative of business and peaceful development is that companies do not serve simply as the engine for jobs and shared prosperity once an enabling environment has been created. Business leaders, in the form of Perlmutter's 'social architects', can through their actions reduce fragility. The private sector within this narrative is an enlightened participant in state-building and good citizenship. International policy responses as a result encourage ever greater business roles in social, economic and political development. The Busan Partnership for Effective Development Cooperation established by representatives of developing and developed countries, for example, is the outcome of the fourth High-Level Forum on Aid Effectiveness in 2011. The Busan Partnership recognises 'the central role of the private sector in advancing innovation, creating wealth, income and jobs, mobilizing domestic resources and in turn contributing to poverty reduction'. It therefore commits 'to enable the participation of the private sector in the design and implementation of development policies and strategies to foster sustainable growth and poverty reduction'.[69]

Building on such presumptions of the goodwill of business, the most prominent international initiatives intend to help private-sector actors navigate complex environments. The UN Global Compact's guidance on responsible business in conflict-affected and high-risk areas notes that 'operating a business unit in a high-risk area poses a number of dilemmas with no easy answers'. It seeks to 'help reduce corporate risks and enhance the capacity of companies to make a positive contribution to peace and development' by encouraging companies to examine and adapt their core business operations, government relations, local stakeholder engagement and strategic social investment to the complexities of fragile states.[70]

A focus on how the business manages its own operations in conflict-prone environments appears to be particularly fruitful for companies. One oil company in Colombia found that its strong employee relations contributed to a 'social protection circle' that helped to create leverage with armed groups, as the guerrillas would inquire of the union whether the company treated workers well.[71] In Egypt, a large-scale dairy processor had its 'best year ever' in the middle of a revolution. Its general manager attributes this in part to its strategic choice to eschew simpler and perhaps less expensive commercial milk operations in favour of sourcing milk from small-scale farmers, who similarly had an interest in protecting the company.[72]

The OECD Guidelines for Multinational Enterprises (MNEs), part of the 1976 OECD Declaration on International Investment and Multinational Enterprises (updated in 2011), 'encourage the positive contribution MNEs can make to economic, social and environmental progress'[73] by providing 'principles and standards for responsible business conduct'[74] across a similar range of issues as the Global Compact. While not focused specifically on fragile or conflict-prone environments, in their 2011 embracing of the Guiding Principles on Business and Human Rights the Guidelines recognise that businesses should act responsibly even where governments fail 'either to enforce relevant domestic laws, or to implement international human rights obligations', or 'act contrary to such laws or international obligations'.[75] The OECD's related projects, including the OECD Due Diligence Guidance for Responsible Supply Chains of Minerals from Conflict-Affected and High-Risk Areas, are promulgated more specifically to help companies 'respect human rights and avoid contributing to conflict'.[76] One study of supply chain initiatives in the eastern Democratic Republic of the Congo pursuant to the Due Diligence Guidance found a notable positive impact on the availability of conflict-free minerals, as well as a reduction in interference by armed non-state actors in many instances.[77]

The countries that adhere to the Guidelines for Multinational Enterprises, which include both OECD and non-OECD members, agree to set up national contact points to promote the Guidelines, receive complaints from any party concerning the conduct of a national company and provide 'a mediation and conciliation platform for resolving issues that may arise' concerning implementation of the Guidelines.[78] Even critics of the OECD contact point mechanism admit that it can be useful in discrete cases, as for example when the Canadian national contact point mediated an agreement with First Quantum Mining to address community resettlement problems linked to its mine in Zambia.[79] But the principles are clear: 'Observance of the Guidelines by enterprises is voluntary and not legally enforceable.'[80] Rather, 'The underlying idea behind this approach is to focus on building an atmosphere of mutual trust between all stakeholders in order to overcome global corporate responsibility challenges'.[81] The OECD argues that 'MNEs have a strong business incentive to act responsibly',[82] apparently obviating any need for more strict regulatory measures. The Global Compact for its part notes that 'In some cases, companies may negatively impact their own operations and their activities may exacerbate conflict or instability – even if their intentions are for the best.'[83] But it similarly takes the perspective there is 'effectively no contradiction between maximized long-term financial performance and positive contributions to peace and development',[84] and reinforces that its principles are also voluntary. Under the narrative of business as an agent for peaceful development, such guidance is not a form of regulation; rather, it assists the company in its difficult task of avoiding conflict and promoting peaceful development.

Companies are increasingly invited into conversations about how they can increase their impact on fragile contexts and development outcomes through their business operations. At the enterprise level, this often involves partnerships that provide significant public and non-profit resources for business expansion. Ajinomoto, for example, is a Japanese food company that in 2015 reported more than US$8 billion in sales in over 130 countries. In 2013 it brought to market in Ghana a food supplement for children, KOKO Plus. According to the Business Call to Action – a platform for business engagement around the Millennium Development Goals supported by bilateral and multilateral donors and hosted by the UNDP – the Japan International Cooperation Agency (JICA) funded the nutrition feasibility study and provided support; the United States Agency for International Development (USAID) supported feasibility studies on the distribution model; and the Global Alliance for Improved Nutrition (GAIN) provided technical expertise in monitoring and evaluation. The NGOs Plan International and CARE take part in nutrition and distribution model studies, and the Ghana Health Service provides outreach to encourage mothers to use the product. GIZ, the German international cooperation agency, is funding a market expansion study. Financial and technical support for the multinational giant to establish itself in the market will continue for up to four years.[85]

At the policy level, large-scale public–private partnerships dominate. The New Alliance for Food Security and Nutrition, launched in 2012 at the G8 summit at Camp David, brings together bilateral and multilateral donors, foundations such as the Rockefeller Foundation and Gates Foundation, the governments of fragile and conflict-affected states such as Burkina Faso, Côte d'Ivoire and Ethiopia, and multinational companies such as Cargill, Syngenta and Yara to discuss policy reforms. Among the New Alliance's initiatives are those 'to build domestic and international private sector confidence to increase agricultural investment significantly'.[86] These may include working with governments to introduce investment incentives and tax benefits for multinationals; reform land tenure to the benefit of large-scale commercial agriculture; and open markets to foreign seed providers.

Although the words 'food security and nutrition' are part of the New Alliance name, many of its projects target non-food crops, including cotton, biofuels, rubber and export crops. This focus on large-scale agribusiness investment as well as the prominent role of multinationals at the policy table have led to strong criticism by some international NGOs and the UN special rapporteur for food security, among others. But such initiatives draw on the narrative of business as an agent for peaceful development to argue that private-sector investment will lead to higher income, improved food security and reduced poverty levels.[87] Whether one agrees or not with this public–private partnership approach, the proliferation of such enterprise and policy-level partnerships makes it hard to argue with the observation that 'The private sector has become the new donor darling.'[88]

Company partnerships may move outside the usual boundaries of the business to tackle problems with which a fragile state cannot, or will not, cope. By 1998, prevalence rates for HIV/AIDS in Zimbabwe, for example, had risen to 27.2%, with almost every family affected by very high mortality rates and other consequences of the disease. The previously well-maintained health care infrastructure collapsed under the weight of the burden of the disease, a growing economic crisis and the migration abroad of many health care professionals. Chronic food insecurity left individuals with compromised immune systems vulnerable to life-threatening opportunistic infections such as tuberculosis. Companies such as Sandvik Mining and Construction Zimbabwe, part of the Sandvik engineering group headquartered in Sweden, began collaboration with the Swedish Workplace HIV/AIDS Programme (SWHAP). The programme, jointly initiated in 2004 by the International

Council of Swedish Industry and the Swedish Industrial and Metalworkers' Union, uses Swedish and Norwegian development funding to develop workplace HIV/AIDS programmes. Sandvik also engaged the Zimbabwe AIDS Prevention and Support Organisation (ZAPSO) to provide technical assistance.

Working with its partners, Sandvik provided food to all employees during the hyperinflation from 2008 to 2009, including nutritional supplements to HIV/AIDS-affected employees. It instituted a voluntary counselling and testing service, and provided free antiretroviral treatment to employees and their families. As its own programme took root, it expanded outreach to companies in its supply chain, helping small suppliers in particular to benefit from its sophisticated programme, and encouraged its large mining customers to engage more consequentially. Sandvik took action to help alleviate a social crisis that greatly affected its people; but it readily articulates the business case for its HIV/AIDS work, with one company poster stating: 'Promote employee wellness. Protect production.'[89] Such initiatives thus sit at the intersection of corporate social investment and enlightened business management. In the narrative of business as an agent for peaceful development, they illustrate how business can act as a catalyst for positive change, meeting both social and company needs in conflict-prone and otherwise fragile environments.

Multinationals in the narrative of business as an agent for peaceful development may step in to fill voids in government regulation or rights enforcement. The Conflict-Free Gold Standard, a unilateral industry initiative of the World Gold Council in London, introduced a system of entirely private oversight of company members' systems and processes for due diligence meant to 'provide assurance that their gold has been extracted in a manner that does not cause, support or benefit unlawful armed conflict or contribute to serious human rights abuses or breaches of international humanitarian law'.[90] In the aftermath of a series of Bangladeshi fires and other tragedies culminating in the garment factory collapse in Dhaka that killed more than 1,100 and injured 2,000 more, international apparel brands and retailers entered into an agreement with Bangladeshi trade unions. This agreement, managed by the Bangladesh Accord Foundation established in the Netherlands in 2013, creates a complex regulatory regime for garment manufacturers in Bangladesh including site inspections, remediation plans, factory-level worker committees, clarifications of workers' rights to refuse unsafe work and grievance mechanisms for workers.[91] In both of the above cases, the regulations concerning company operations in the conflict-prone or otherwise fragile environment are written and managed from European capitals. This is done in whole or in part by multinational companies in the absence of a host state government that is legitimate, capable or willing enough to implement such a regulatory regime itself.

Multinationals may also address the challenges of a corrupt state. The G20 Anti-Corruption Action Plan 2013–2014, a follow-up to the first G20 Anti-Corruption Action Plan concluded in Seoul in 2011, declares that 'Business is an important stakeholder in anti-corruption efforts ... We reiterate our support for public–private partnerships to combat corruption,' for example the Extractive Industries Transparency Initiative (EITI) and the Construction Sector Transparency Initiative (CoST).[92] The UNDP recognises the role of the private sector (among other role players) 'in exposing corruption, putting pressure on enforcement, and promoting transparency and accountability', noting a particular role in 'macro and micro economic policy settings'.[93] Such initiatives tell a story of corporate solidarity with civil society to hold governments accountable.

In extreme cases, a company can become the guarantor of stability. Independent reports, for example, have consistently noted the positive influence of Total in the operations area of its Yadana pipeline in Myanmar, intervening with the government and military to address forced labour and other human rights issues, and helping to maintain a degree of normality that stands in stark contrast to other regions of the country. At the same time, it maintained its licence to operate in the face of fierce international criticism by those advocating total divestment from Myanmar.[94]

Meanwhile, Chevron, the third-largest oil producer in Nigeria with operations based in the Niger Delta, became a force for greater stability in that region. In the past:

> Grievances from Delta communities were often dealt with in military terms, resulting in severe violations of human rights. ... [I]njustice and poverty gave rise to an armed militant movement that, until recently, targeted both government and oil industry facilities and operations. ... In 2003, the western area of the Niger Delta descended into a bloody and destructive inter-ethnic conflict, fueled in part by increasing competition over mineral rights, and the associated benefits that communities and individuals hoped to reap.[95]

Noting that its approach to community relations was utterly failing to manage operational disruptions, theft, extortion and increasingly high levels of violence against the company, Chevron took a new approach that established local governance over community development where it had not existed before. Now, Regional Development Councils – comprising clusters of communities – engage Chevron, as well as all levels of government and development actors, to set priorities and implement their own projects. Chevron, a founding member of the Voluntary Principles on Security and Human Rights, a 'set of principles designed to guide companies in maintaining the safety and security of their operations within an operating framework that encourages respect for human rights',[96] used its influence to moderate the government's militarised response to conflict. Chevron's approach – mitigating corrupt and even hostile government – has had a demonstrable effect on development outcomes and the reduction of violence for communities in the Niger Delta. It has also notably reduced the level of violence and disruption levelled at Chevron.[97] Drawing from the logic of such examples, the UN Global Compact argues that 'Business can be a powerful agent of change.'[98]

Enabling business to address conflict in fragile states

As in the previous chapter on the narrative of the predatory multinational company, the goal here is not to provide a comprehensive inventory of the intellectual roots or policy expressions of the narrative of business as a foundation for peaceful development; neither is it to evaluate the extent to which the narrative is generally true or untrue across time and geographies. Rather, the chapter shows that the positive narrative of business and peace also has a long and unbroken history that results in distinct international policy expressions; such expressions are in this case more strongly supported by national governments and multilateral institutions, and are more deeply embedded in international financial and development policy regimes.

The common thread running through these policies is the presumption that deprivation is at the heart of much protracted conflict and violence. The premise that foreign investment will reduce conflict leads to the conclusion that creating an enabling environment for business should be made a high priority in conflict-prone environments. Over the last two decades, international policy has increasingly migrated from a more passive view of the benefits of a liberal economy to the active promotion of business as an agent for shaping the fragile state. The proposed solution to conflict is to bring more and more of society into a liberal economy through state-building, liberal market reforms and enlightened private-sector mindsets.

The examples given in Chapters One and Two underline that both the narrative of the predatory multinational company and the narrative of business as a foundation for peaceful development are demonstrably rooted in long history and real experience. There are companies that act with shocking disregard for human life and human dignity, and with apparent impunity. There are also those that out of enlightened self-interest engage differently in fragile states to advance both business and social goals.

What is perhaps surprising, therefore, is the degree to which the two dominant discourses fail to intersect or engage with one another. An example of this disconnect can be found in the World Bank's *World Development Report 2011: Conflict, Security and Development*.[99] The report highlights the cost to business of conflict, noting that 'Insecurity takes a significant toll on the private sector'.[100] It presents a vision of a private sector as an island of stability in an otherwise hostile environment, claiming that 'Private sector activity often cuts across ethnic and religious lines, where rules-based competition is the cornerstone. Violence shortens the time horizons of consumers, producers, traders, and policy makers. Outreach to the private sector can help build a sense of the long term, which is critical for planning, investment in the future, and sustainable growth.'[101] It strongly advocates business incentives because, 'In violent situations … creating the right environment for businesses is often not enough to attract investment; more direct intervention is needed for the private sector to play its catalytic role'.[102] In the report's world view, business is effective in reducing corruption[103] – indeed, business is needed to provide capacities for audit and inspection to combat corruption[104] and in 'monitoring' other government reforms;[105] furthermore, self-regulation by industry groups in multi-stakeholder partnerships is working.[106] The report concludes that: 'A bolder approach could draw together capacities from development agencies, the private sector, foundations, and nongovernmental organizations (NGOs) to support a new global partnership to galvanize investments in countries and communities where high unemployment and social disengagement contribute to the risks of conflict.'[107]

Yet in the entire *World Development Report*, the term 'private sector' appears on 51 pages, but never in the context of the predatory multinational company that may exploit fragility, or the possible negative impacts – intentional or not – of private foreign investment on conflict or violence. In the same vein, the word 'regulation' appears on 15 pages, but never with the suggestion that, in some cases, enhanced regulation or accountability of private enterprise could contribute to reducing conflict. In an attempt perhaps to skirt the shadow of the Washington Consensus altogether, the report simply avoids the words 'liberal' or 'liberalisation' throughout. Similarly, a report on the 'role of mining in national economies' by the International Council on Mining and Metals – an industry association that espouses among other principles the upholding of fundamental human rights – asserts that 'it is clear that mining can make a contribution that translates to greater well-being for the people'. However, the report fails to make a single reference to any negative impact of mining on national economies or local communities, even in fragile states.[108] The discourses of business and conflict and of business and peace, as well as their international policy initiatives, occur largely in parallel universes.

Notes

1   Robert O. Collins and James M. Burns, *A History of Sub-Saharan Africa* (Cambridge: Cambridge University Press, 2007), p. 346.

2   Merle Lipton, *Capitalism and Apartheid: South Africa, 1910–1986* (Aldershot: Wildwood House, 1986), p. 119.

3   *Ibid.*, p. 134.

4   *Ibid.*, p. 229.

5   Gay W. Seidman, *Manufacturing Militance: Workers' Movements in Brazil and South Africa, 1970–1985* (Berkeley: University of California Press, 1994), p. 135.

6   Philip Hirschsohn, 'Negotiating a Democratic Order: Learning from Mediation and Industrial Relations', *Negotiation Journal*, vol. 12, no. 2, 1996, p. 142.

7   Joseph Lelyveld, 'The Many Faces of Barlow Rand Ltd', *New York Times*, 11 April 1982.

8   Nel Marais and Jo Davies, *The Role of the Business Elite in South Africa's Democratic Transition: Supporting an Inclusive Political and Economic Transformation* (Berlin: Berghof Foundation, 2015).

9   John Locke, *Second Treatise* (1689).

10 John S. Mill, *Principles of Political Economy* (London: Hackett, 1848), p. 582.

11 Howard V. Perlmutter, 'The Tortuous Evolution of the Multinational Corporation', *Columbia Journal of World Business*, vol. 4, no. 1, 1969, pp. 9–10.

12 Erik Gartzke, *Economic Freedom and Peace. Economic Freedom of the World – 2005 Annual Report* (Vancouver: The Fraser Institute, 2005), p. 34.

13 *Ibid.*, p. 39.

14 Thomas L. Friedman, *The Lexus and the Olive Tree* (New York: Anchor, 1990), p. 248.

15 Thomas L. Friedman, *The World is Flat: A Brief History of the Twenty-First Century* (New York: Farrar, Straus and Giroux, 2005), p. 421.

16 Michael Doyle, 'Three Pillars of the Liberal Peace', *American Political Science Review*, vol. 99, no. 3, 2006, p. 466.

17 Roland Paris, 'Peacebuilding and the Limits of Liberal Internationalism', *International Security*, vol. 22, no. 2, 1997, p. 56.

18 Articles of Agreement of the International Monetary Fund, adopted 22 July 1944, https://www.imf.org/external/pubs/ft/aa/#intro.

19 Dominique Strauss-Kahn, 'Economic Stability, Economic Cooperation, and Peace – The Role of the IMF', Remarks at the Global Creative Leadership Summit, New York City, 2009.

20 IBRD Articles of Agreement, http://siteresources.worldbank.org/EXTABOUTUS/Resources/ibrd-articlesofagreement.pdf.

21 IDA Articles of Agreement, http://www.worldbank.org/ida/articles-agreement/IDA-articles-of-agreement.pdf.

22 John Williamson, 'A Short History of the Washington Consensus', in Narcís Serra and Joseph E. Stiglitz (eds.), *The Washington Consensus Reconsidered: Towards a New Global Governance* (Oxford: Oxford University Press, 2008), pp. 14–30.

23 History and quotations from World Bank sources: http://www.ifc.org/wps/wcm/connect/CORP_EXT_Content/IFC_External_Corporate_Site/About+IFC/IFC+History.

24 *Ibid.*

25 African Development Bank Group (ADBG), *Supporting the Transformation of the Private Sector in Africa: Private Sector Development Strategy, 2013–2017* (Tunis: ADBG, 2013).

26 Karl Wohlmuth, *Good Governance and Economic Development: New Foundations for Growth in Africa* (Bremen: Universität Bremen, 1998), p. 13.

27 IFC, *Improving Lives: IDA & Conflict-Affected Areas – Creating Opportunity in Strife-Torn Environments*, Annual Report, 2015 Online Report (2015).

28 IFC, *Telling Our Story: Frontier Focus* (Washington, DC: IFC, 2011), p. 12.

29 IFC, *Final Report on CASA's First Cycle (2008–2013)* (Washington, DC: IFC, 2014), p. 7.

30 United Nations Conference on Trade and Development (UNCTAD) data. Accessed 14 January 2016 at http://investmentpolicyhub.unctad.org/IIA.

31 Hermann Abs and Hartley Shawcross, 'The Proposed Convention to Protect Private Foreign Investment: Introduction', *Journal of Public Law*, vol. 9, no. 1, 1960, p. 115.

32 International Centre for the Settlement of Investment Disputes (ICSID), *The ICSID Caseload: Statistics – Issue 2013–2* (Washington, DC: ICSID, 2013).

33 MIGA, *2008 Annual Report* (Washington, DC: MIGA, 2008), p. 5.

34 David Gaukrodger, *Investment Treaties and Shareholder Claims: Analysis of Treaty Practice* (Paris: OECD, 2014), p. 3.

35 Fourth Report of the Independent Expert on the Promotion of a Democratic and Equitable International Order, Alfred-Maurice de Zayas, Submitted in Accordance with Assembly Resolution 69/178. A/70/285 (2015), p. 13.

36 Blacksmith Institute, *The World's Worst Polluted Places: The Top Ten of the Dirty Thirty* (New York: Blackstone Institute, 2007), pp. 24–5.

37 Kenneth J. Vandevelde, 'The Economics of Bilateral Investment Treaties', *Harvard International Law Journal*, vol. 41, no. 2, 2000, p. 499.

38 Zachary Elkins, Andrew T. Guzman and Beth A. Simmons, *Competing for Capital: The Diffusion of Bilateral Investment Treaties, 1960–2000*, working paper, University of Illinois, University of California at Berkeley and Harvard University (2004), p. 4.

39 Elliot Berg, *Accelerated Development in Sub-Saharan Africa: A Plan for Action* (Washington, DC: IBRD, 1981).

40 Wohlmuth, *Good Governance and Economic Development*.

41 *Ibid.*, p. 38.

42 *Ibid.*, p. 41.

43 *Ibid.*, p. 42.

44 African Development Bank (AfDB), *Addressing Fragility and Building*

Resilience in Africa: The African Development Bank Group Strategy 2014–2019 (Tunis: AfDB, 2014), p. 9.

45 Joseph E. Stiglitz, 'Is There a Post-Washington Consensus Consensus?', in Serra and Stiglitz, The Washington Consensus Reconsidered, pp. 41–56, at p. 41.

46 Ibid., p. 43.

47 John Williamson, 'What Should the World Bank Think About the Washington Consensus?', World Bank Research Observer, vol. 15, no. 2, 2000, p. 262.

48 Stiglitz, 'Is There a Post-Washington Consensus Consensus?', p. 43.

49 Williamson, 'A Short History of the Washington Consensus', p. 27.

50 Craig Burnside and David Dollar, Aid, the Incentive Regime, and Poverty Reduction, Policy Research Working Paper 1937 (Washington, DC: World Bank, 1998).

51 Robert Wade, 'Japan, the World Bank, and the Art of Paradigm Maintenance: The East Asian Miracle in Political Perspective', New Left Review, no. 217, 1996, pp. 3–36; Alice Amsden, Jacek Kochanowicz, and Lance Taylor, The Market Meets its Match: Restructuring the Economies of Eastern Europe (Cambridge, MA: Harvard University Press, 1994).

52 Independent Evaluation Group (IEG), Engaging with Fragile States: An IEG Review of World Bank Support to Low-Income Countries Under Stress (Washington, DC: IEG, 2006), p. xxii.

53 Organisation for Economic Co-operation and Development (OECD), 'Monitoring the Principles for Good International Engagement in Fragile States and Situations' (Paris: OECD, 2007), p. 22.

54 World Bank, World Development Report 2011: Conflict, Security and Development (Washington, DC: World Bank, 2011), pp. xi–xii.

55 IDA Resource Mobilization Department, IDA's Support to Fragile and Conflict-Affected States (Washington, DC: World Bank Group, 2013), p. 2.

56 African Legal Support Facility, 'Agreement for the Establishment of the African Legal Support Facility', http://www.afdb.org/fileadmin/uploads/afdb/Documents/Legal-Documents/Agreement%20for%20the%20Establishment%20of%20the%20African%20Legal%20Support%20Facility%20(ALSF).pdf.

57 World Bank and United Nations Environment Programme (UNEP), Expert Consultation: Geo-mapping Extractive Resources in g7+ Fragile States (Washington, DC and Geneva: World Bank and UNEP, 2013).

58 United Nations, A New Global Partnership: Eradicate Poverty and Transform Economies through Sustainable Development (New York: United Nations, 2013), p. 9.

59 Dani Rodrik, 'Goodbye Washington Consensus, Hello Washington Confusion? A Review of the World Bank's "Economic Growth in the 1990s: Learning from a Decade of Reform"', Journal of Economic Literature, vol. 44, no. 4, 2006, pp. 974, 979.

60 Fund for Peace, Fragile State Index (2015), http://fsi.fundforpeace.org.

61 Brian Ganson, Risk and Risk Mitigation in the Oil and Gas Sector in Uganda (Geneva: Geneva Peacebuilding Platform, 2012).

62 Ibid.

63 OECD, 'Freedom of Investment at the OECD', http://www.oecd.org/

daf/inv/investment-policy/foi.htm.

64 World Bank, *World Development Report 2011*, p. 80.

65 Jenick Rodan, 'How to Negotiate an Oil Agreement', in Macartan Humphreys, Jeffrey D. Sachs, and Joseph E. Stiglitz (eds), *Escaping the Resource Curse* (New York: Columbia University Press, 2007), pp. 89–113.

66 Brian Ganson, 'How Do We Put all the Pieces Together: Tetra Leval's Food for Development Office', in Brian Ganson (ed.), *Management in Complex Environments: Questions for Leaders* (Stockholm: International Council of Swedish Industry, 2013), pp. 158–65.

67 See Fragile States Index 2015, http://ffp.statesindex.org.

68 See http://www.transparency.org/country#BGD.

69 OECD, *Fourth High Level Forum On Aid Effectiveness: Busan Partnership For Effective Development Co-Operation* (Paris: OECD, 2011), p. 10.

70 United Nations Global Compact (UNGC) and Principles for Responsible Investment, *Guidance on Responsible Business in Conflict-Affected and High-Risk Areas: A Resource for Companies and Investors* (New York: UNGC, 2010), p. 1.

71 Luc Zandvliet, Yezid Campos Zornosa, and David Reyes, *Efforts to Operate Constructively in a Context of Conflict: Best Corporate Practices in Colombia* (Cambridge, MA: CDA, 2004), p. 46.

72 Interview by Brian Ganson.

73 OECD, *OECD Guidelines for Multinational Enterprises* (Paris: OECD, 2011), p. 7.

74 *Ibid.*, p. 3.

75 *Ibid.*, p. 32.

76 OECD, *OECD Due Diligence Guidance for Responsible Supply Chains of Minerals from Conflict-Affected and High-Risk Areas* (Paris: OECD, 2013).

77 International Peace Information Service, *Mineral Supply Chains and Conflict Links in Eastern Democratic Republic of Congo: Five Years of Implementing Supply Chain Due Diligence* (Paris: OECD, 2015).

78 OECD, *OECD Guidelines for Multinational Enterprises*, p. 3.

79 Joris Oldenziel, Joseph Wilde-Ramsing and Patricia Feeney, *10 Years On: Assessing the Contribution of the OECD Guidelines for Multinational Enterprises to Responsible Business Conduct* (The Hague: OECD Watch, 2010), p. 12.

80 OECD, *OECD Guidelines for Multinational Enterprises*, p. 17.

81 *Ibid.*, p. 3.

82 *Ibid.*

83 UN Global Compact and PRI, *Guidance on Responsible Business in Conflict-Affected and High-Risk Areas*, p. 6.

84 *Ibid.*, p. 2.

85 Ai Ohara, *Ajinomoto Co.: Better Nutrition, Brighter Future in Ghana* (New York: Business Call to Action, 2013).

86 See New Alliance for Food Security and Nutrition, 'Cooperation Framework to Support the New Alliance for Food Security and Nutrition in Mozambique' (2012), p. 2.

87 Claire Provost, Liz Ford and Mark Tran, 'G8 New Alliance Condemned as New Wave of Colonialism in Africa', *Guardian*, 18 February 2014.

88 Shannon Kindornay and Fraser Reilly-King, *Investing in the Business*

of Development: Bilateral Donor Approaches to Engaging the Private Sector (Ottawa: The North-South Institute and Canadian Council for International Co-operation, 2013), p. 1.

89 Paul Hollesen, 'How Can We Be the Catalyst for Change? Sandvik Mining and Construction Zimbabwe's Wellness Programme', in Ganson, Management in Complex Environments, pp. 50–7.

90 World Gold Council (WGC), Conflict Free Gold Standard (London: WGC, 2012), p. 1.

91 Accord on Fire and Building Safety in Bangladesh, 13 May 2013, http://bangladeshaccord.org/wp-content/uploads/2013/10/the_accord.pdf.

92 See http://www.oecd.org/daf/anti-bribery/G20_Anti-Corruption_Action_Plan_(2013-2014).pdf.

93 UNDP, UNDP Global Anti-Corruption Initiative (GAIN) 2014–2017 (New York: UNDP, 2014), pp. 17, 18.

94 The series of reports by CDA from 2002 to 2015 are available at http://www.cdacollaborative.org/publications.

95 Merrick Hoben, David Kovick, David Plumb, and Justin Wright, Corporate and Community Engagement in the Niger Delta: Lessons Learned from Chevron Nigeria Limited's GMOU Process (Cambridge, MA: Consensus Building Institute, 2012), p. 2.

96 http://www.voluntaryprinciples.org.

97 Ibid.

98 UNGC, Business for Peace (New York: UNGC, 2013), p. 5.

99 World Bank, World Development Report 2011.

100 Ibid., p. 65.

101 Ibid., p. 122.

102 Ibid., p. 157.

103 Ibid., p. 158.

104 Ibid., p. 258.

105 Ibid., p. 249.

106 Ibid., p. 286.

107 Ibid., p. 274.

108 ICMM, The Role of Mining in National Economies (London: ICMM, 2014), p. 3.

CHAPTER THREE

The changing landscape of business and conflict in fragile states

Myanmar provides examples that can be claimed both by those telling the story of the predatory multinational company at the root of violence, and by those telling the story of the private sector as a foundation for peaceful development. Those attracted to the former discourse highlight the findings of the US federal tribunal, summarised in Chapter One, that found Union Oil Company of California (Unocal) complicit in gross human rights abuses, including forced labour and murder, in the construction of the Yadana pipeline (completed in 1998), and claim ongoing abuses of the same nature.[1] Those more sympathetic to the latter discourse can cite an independent report, written a decade later, finding that there were no community voices within the pipeline area, by that time managed by Total Oil, who wanted the company to leave; Total's presence was by and large felt to be a source of security and welcome development assistance in the face of an authoritarian and abusive military regime.[2]

The policy responses arising from these respective world views are to some extent predictable. The Burma Campaign and EarthRights International call for the international investigation of corporate crimes as well as the placing of severe restrictions on foreign investment in Myanmar, for example, the halting of all dam construction projects.[3] Meanwhile, the Myanmar Centre for Responsible Business, supported by a variety of bilateral and multilateral donors and headed by a former UK ambassador to Myanmar, works to 'encourage responsible business activities throughout Myanmar'[4] through education on, and promotion of, international standards. In Myanmar we see the global discourse replicated in a specific national context.

Such examples, however, paint an incomplete picture of business and conflict in this fragile state. Myanmar suffers a high rate of deforestation, estimated at about 1% per year between 1990 and 2010,[5] with certain species such as rosewood facing extinction.[6] This is in part driven by illegal logging exports to Thailand, Vietnam, China and elsewhere,[7] and in part by the large-scale allocation of forest lands by the government for commercial agriculture, the effect of which is to displace small-holders and fuel conflict. In the mining sector, local protests against land takings for the development of the Letpadaung copper mine by Wanbao Mining of China and the Myanmar military's business arm in 2012 were suppressed with 'white phosphorus smoke bombs, usually reserved for warfare'; in 2014 'police officers opened fire on residents who were protesting evictions in the area, killing one woman with a shot to the head'.[8] This is in addition to clashes among organised non-state armed groups for the control of minerals in areas not under the rule of the central government.

Moreover, where some saw the boiling over of long-standing religious conflict in the anti-Muslim violence of 2012, others saw ethnic cleansing by the Myanmar army as being tied more to 'competition for scarce land and resources'[9] and attempts to divert attention from deeply unpopular projects; one such project was the construction of the 1,100-km pipeline from the new deep water port at Kyaukphyu in Rakhine State to Kunming, the capital of China's Yunnan province. Meanwhile, young men are trafficked from Myanmar to become slaves on Thai fishing vessels as well as in processing facilities.[10] All of this takes place in an environment characterised by deep distrust between ethnic groups, between the central and regional governments, between civilian and military authorities, between civil society and government, between those focused on technocratic government and those on security, between those more and less committed to the various negotiated ceasefires, between those suffering acute deprivation and those better off, between the landed and the unlanded rural poor, and even between older and younger generations.[11]

It is increasingly clear that these complex and turbulent dynamics represent the new strategic landscape confronted by international businesses in fragile states. United Nations Development Programme (UNDP) data from 2011 found '87 countries in all of the world's regions ... facing the prospects of potential violence, prolonged deadlock, or a relapse into violent conflict over the next two to three-year period'.[12] From the vista of 2016, this assessment has proven largely accurate as evidenced by developments in North and Central Africa and the Middle East as well as the persistence of criminal violence in Central and South America. A multinational company entering into a fragile state therefore becomes part of a multi-dimensional and highly stressed system. It may cause conflict directly, but it may also exacerbate latent conflicts in which the multinational corporation is only one role player among many, or it may become caught up in conflicts not at all of the company's own making.

It is less clear how the two dominant international discourses on business in fragile states address such diverse presentations of conflict and violence or the variety of ways in which companies become caught up in them. Built on historical foundations of inter- and intra-state violence in the Cold War period, both discourses assume that actors are responsive to incentives and disincentives at the global level. Contemporary international focus on the negative or positive behaviour of multinational corporations – and in particular those within reach of multilateral financial institutions and Western policymakers – is therefore too narrow to address the multi-faceted and intertwined dynamics of business and conflict in fragile states. And even when international policy approaches attempt to engage a wider range of actors or dynamics, they do so at international and national levels far removed from any particular context. Contemporary attempts to manage business and conflict in fragile states are therefore incapable of reaching the necessary range of actors or address-ing the dynamics at the heart of conflict and its resolution in a particular time and place.

The increasingly local face of conflict

As Chapters One and Two illustrate, old understandings of the relationship between business and conflict in fragile states, rooted in centuries of history, strongly influence contempo-rary policy and practice. The same is true for notions of conflict itself. Much of contemporary international policy operates within a long-standing framework in which conflict is defined as conventional fights – between governments or between governments and rebel groups – to win control over territory and resources. The standard international definition of armed conflict, codified in humanitarian law beginning with the 1864 Geneva Convention, refers to 'international armed conflicts, opposing two or more States, and non-international armed conflicts, between governmental forces and non-governmental armed groups, or between such groups only ... Legally speaking, no other type of armed conflict exists.'[13]

This framework is also at the root of many international institutions. The very term 'United Nations' came into broad use with the 1942 'Declaration by United Nations', signed by 26 countries. It asserted that 'complete victory over their enemies is essential to defend life, liberty, independence and religious freedom'. The countries invited to the 1945 San Francisco Conference establishing the United Nations we know today included only those that had declared war on Germany and Japan.[14] The United Nations Charter – as the Bretton Woods institutions discussed in Chapter Two – oriented the institution towards the realities of that time: 'the scourge of war, which twice in our lifetime has brought untold sorrow to mankind'.[15] While this persistent state-centric framework is not immutable – under UN Secretary-General Boutros Boutros-Ghali, for example, the UN through its 1992 Agenda for Peace recognised a new strategic landscape after the Cold War in which intra-state armed conflict played a more important role[16] – it has its roots in nineteenth-century warfare where uniformed soldiers of state armies confront each other on the field of battle.

This understanding also shaped the study of conflict. In the 1960s, David Singer and Melvin Small pioneered the Correlates of War Project at the University of Michigan, a study of the history of interstate warfare since 1816. To be included, a war needed to have at least two parties (of which one was required to be a government) and to lead to at least 1,000 battle deaths. This work built on a state-centric understanding of international relations within an international system of states.[17] The project reflected a broader trend to apply scientific approaches to the social sciences.[18] It inspired decades of research on conflict by economists and political scientists who found in the 'state' and 'rebel group' unitary actors whose interactions could be studied, explained and predicted. The Uppsala Conflict Data Program, for example, an influential source of data on armed conflict, defines armed conflict as 'a contested incompatibility which concerns government and/or territory where the use of armed force between two parties, of which at least one is the government of a state, results in at least 25 battle-related deaths'.[19] Using this definition, in 2014 it reported 40 armed conflicts, 11 of which were major wars,[20] resulting in around 100,000 deaths. By the 1990s, such approaches to the study of war had become influential among policymakers. The focus on states and rebel groups corresponded to the types of conflicts relevant for multilateral organisations and states, and scientific approaches were perceived by policymakers to make a more powerful case for policy recommendations.[21]

Much of the response to conflict by multilateral institutions remains within this framework of inter- and intra-state war. The UN Security Council in 2014–2015 focused notably on Yemen, Syria and African conflicts that matched traditional conceptions of war.[22] The UN Peacebuilding Commission currently operates under a model in which the countries on its agenda – Burundi, the Central African Republic, Guinea, Guinea-Bissau, Liberia and Sierra Leone – are considered 'post conflict' in light of formal agreements purporting to end armed conflict. Multilateral resources allocated for humanitarian response to conflict and violence similarly flow towards inter- and intra-state wars. The 2016 consolidated appeal by the UN's Office for the Coordination of Humanitarian Affairs (OCHA), for instance, focuses three-quarters of the US$20.9 billion raised on six war-affected countries: Syria, Iraq, South Sudan, Yemen, Ethiopia and Somalia. The appeal for Syria alone accounts for about US$8bn.[23] These figures illustrate how even the UN's humanitarian response concentrates on contexts affected by inter- or intra-state warfare.

A narrow focus on armed conflict, however, is increasingly out of sync with an era in which instability has become the new normal. Events in Syria, Ukraine or Yemen remind us that wars have important global security implications. Still, the majority of conflicts in fragile states – and especially those relevant to business – occur outside contexts shaped by inter- or intrastate war. Rather, they occur in situations of chronic violence[24] or turbulent political transitions that are shaped by a different set of dynamics:

> violent instability as a result of the impact of local and cross-border organized crime; urban violence, as the pace of urbanization continues to accelerate; deep and rapid political change as societies transform themselves after decades of stasis; violent conflict arising from deep, long term divisions, often based on longstanding issues such as land disputes, and often exacerbated by political rivalries; the negative impact on fragile governments of a growing list of external stress factors, from the continuing economic crisis to the effects of climate change; [and] distortion of local priorities driven by the perceived security needs of other actors.[25]

The differences between state-centric and more holistic understandings of conflict are underlined by a look at the geography of violence. On a per capita basis, the world's most violent countries, apart from contemporary Syria, are in Central America: the rate of violent deaths in Honduras stands at 90.4 victims per 100,000 population per year, for example, with Venezuela at 72.2. These rates far exceed those of countries considered to be at war, such as South Sudan (27.4 per 100,000), Iraq (25.8) and Yemen (16.4).[26] Particularly violent countries include investment destinations such as South Africa, Brazil,

Mexico, Panama and Botswana.[27] Yet such countries are invisible through a lens that prioritises inter-state and civil wars. Indeed, of the 30 countries with the highest violent death rates in 2012 (the last year for which comparable data is available), only nine appear on the Uppsala Conflict Data Program list of armed conflicts.[28]

A focus on inter- and intra-state wars distorts understanding not only of where conflict takes place, but also of the nature of its victims and perpetrators. Only about one in ten violent deaths in the world today is the result of organised armed violence between soldiers in uniform or between armies and insurgents; three-quarters of violent deaths occur due to intentional homicide.[29] Globally, criminal violence results in the deaths of more than ten times as many people as terrorism each year.[30] Victims of violence are disproportionately young: the United Nations Office on Drugs and Crime (UNODC) suggests that the most frequent homicide victims globally are young men between 15 and 25 years of age.[31] The Geneva Declaration estimates that 60,000 women and girls were killed violently every year from 2007–2012. This represented only 16% of all intentional homicides committed during this period globally,[32] but approximately half of these murders were committed by intimate partners or family members, compared to fewer than 6% when victims were male.[33] These more nuanced realities of conflict and violence are lost in the dominant international policy focus on wars and insurgencies.

As illustrated in the discussion above, much of the measurement of conflict and violence focuses on deaths. Yet fatalities 'are only a fraction of the health and social burden arising from violence', according to the World Health Organization.[34] The scale of non-lethal consequences of violence becomes especially clear when considering physical, sexual and psychological abuse, particularly of women and children. One-quarter of all adults report having been physically abused as children; one in five women reports having been sexually abused as a child; one in three women has been a victim of physical or sexual violence by an intimate partner at some point in her lifetime; and one in 17 older adults reports abuse in the past month.[35] Companies are indirectly affected as these dynamics of violence affect employees, their family members and neighbours in both developed and frontier markets.

Non-lethal conflict and violence also have important direct consequences for business. In Mexico, for example, survey data indicated that the most prominent type of criminal attack is armed robbery, affecting 23% of the businesses polled. Other crimes relate to theft by employees and extortion. Industrial firms listed harassment by corrupt officials as the chief source of criminal losses.[36] And, as noted in the Introduction, community and labour conflict and violence can quickly result in losses measured in the tens and even hundreds of millions of dollars from property destruction, idled assets and project abandonments. Conflict and violence related to business in fragile environments takes many forms.

What this broader landscape of conflict shares with inter- and intra-state wars is its functional patterns. Much reporting and analysis suggests that violence is inevitable, that it is deeply rooted in the human psyche, as popularly portrayed in the media.[37] Even Albert Einstein, in his correspondence with Sigmund Freud, wrote that war is possible 'Because man has within him a lust for hatred and destruction'.[38] Yet more than two decades of conflict research establish that violence is the result of planned, purposeful action. As mad as violence may seem, it is almost always utilised to achieve some goal and as part of a broader strategy.[39]

Motivations for violence can be manifold and may be psychological, political, social, or economic.[40] In the context of contested elections, for instance, a local politician may hand out 'scotch and stones' to a loyal youth group to keep opposition voters at home. Violence against a company may be driven by a desire to extract a benefit from it, whether this be a larger community investment fund or a contract for protection services. At the personal level, armed violence has been associated with attempts to feed feelings of impunity, excitement or self-aggrandisement.[41] Violence may even be a function of the fragility of the state itself: for example, increases in lynchings and other forms of vigilante justice in Mexico – against alleged criminals as well as police – are described as 'born of a sense of hopelessness and impotence shared by many in Mexico, where 98% of murders go unsolved and the state is virtually absent in some areas'.[42]

'Part of the problem with much existing analysis,' argues London School of Economics professor David Keen, 'is that conflict continues to be regarded as simply a breakdown in a particular system rather than as the emergence of an alternative system of profit, power and even protection.'[43] Only by understanding these functions of conflict and violence can interveners identify the underlying organisational aspects and motives of conflict that need to be understood and dealt with to nurture its prevention, diffusion and resolution.[44]

The nature of the vast majority of conflict and violence, combined with its purposeful underpinnings, underlines the fact that violence has a strong local dimension. This is true even if it is embedded in broader conflict dynamics.[45] Certainly, global and national factors help to explain the structural context in which violence occurs. Global factors include economic shocks; the radicalisation of religious movements; the link between population pressures and migration; natural and man-made disasters; and, in some contexts, transnational organised crime.[46] At the national level class divisions and land conflicts create an enabling environment for violence. And yet these global and national contextual factors tell us very little about the triggers of violence in a specific context: which individual or business will be targeted and which spared, with what ultimate purpose in mind. As noted in Chapter Two, one oil company in Colombia might be left alone while another is targeted by guerrillas, while in Egypt one company could flourish while others flounder, although all companies in each place operated under the same conditions of civil unrest or war. Indeed, there are well-documented cases of communities that 'opt out' of broader conflicts,[47] highlighting the fact that other cases at some level represent affirmative decisions to 'opt in' to pursue some localised goal. Conflict and violence are highly sensitive to specific local actors and factors of fragility. This means that business and conflict will present in different forms in different places, and for different enterprises in the same places.

The changing strategic landscape of conflict

A look into the future of conflict in fragile states suggests much cause for concern. The Uppsala data might from one perspective be considered relatively good news: the figure of about 100,000 people who died in armed conflicts in 2014 – roughly half of those being in Syria – is relatively low compared to the number of fatalities from large-scale wars of the twentieth century.[48] Indeed, the *Human Security Report 2013* takes note of proponents of a 'declinist thesis', arguing that violence has declined over the centuries.[49] A consistent message across risk forecasts, however, is that a variety of local, national and transnational factors will create more pressures on already fragile states. Such pressures will lead to more conflict, both violent and non-violent,[50] with even non-violent conflict being frequently at a stage of escalation that, if not recognised and addressed, could lead to heightened threats, or to the application, of violence.[51] As stated in October 2015 by Peter Maurer, President of the International Committee of the Red Cross (ICRC), 'We have entered a new era, and it is not a peaceful one.'[52]

Such assessments build on an understanding of the already significant stress factors in fragile environments that will become even more pronounced conflict drivers in the future. Population growth is one such factor. United Nations forecasts suggest that the world population will reach between 8.3bn and 10.9bn people by 2050, with 9.6bn as a mid-projection.[53] This population growth will occur predominantly in the 49 least developed countries, where populations are expected to double from 900 million today to 1.8bn in 2050.[54] Population pressures will manifest themselves differently in different regions, but will almost always provide new sources of conflict at the same time as they exacerbate existing ones. For example, East African societies are likely to see a doubling of populations by 2050, meaning that the majority of the population will be under 15 years old.[55] In the context of highly agriculturally based societies, such a population growth is incongruent with the available land for agriculture, making long-standing land disputes all the more acute. Moreover, as small land-holding plots become increasingly unsustainable and can no longer feed even a single family, migration increases into nearby cities or neighbouring countries, where competition for jobs and opportunities creates new sources of tension.

Population pressures further foster conflict as marginalised young people have access neither to land, nor to alternative jobs.[56] In the context of the brutal civil wars that spread across West Africa, it has been noted that 'Hyper-mobile impoverished rural youth are not a sufficient cause of armed conflict, but their availability for recruitment when other employment opportunities fail is a major factor in fuelling insurgency.'[57]

Multinational corporations along with the governments of many developing countries focus on the 'pursuit of agriculture-led growth as a main strategy to achieve targets on food and nutrition security and shared prosperity',[58] with African heads of state declaring their intent 'to create job opportunities for at least 30% of the youth in agricultural value chains'.[59] But it is less clear how the current focus on large-scale commercial agriculture and its attendant mechanisation will meet these goals, or how the relatively slow speed of implementation can address growing challenges.

From a global perspective, it is cities that will experience the most conflict and violence. With more than 50% of the world's population now living in urban areas – and an estimated 66% by 2050[60] – conflict resolution, violence reduction and peace-building must happen in cities, if at all. Cities remain sites of great poverty and inequality in access to services, including all of the basics: housing, schooling, health care, food, transport, security and justice.[61] In many poorer neighbourhoods and slums, concentrated deprivation goes hand-in-hand with high levels of violence. Analysts of 'fragile cities' – one expression of fragility on a sub-national scale – see the potential for chronic and intense forms of violence to spread from these neighbourhoods to other city areas or intermediate towns, especially in cases where the state has lost the monopoly of force and where there is a failure in the social contract between the government and local citizens.[62] For instance, in Rio de Janeiro, Brazil, drug trafficking groups and para-state militias have become the dominant actors in some of the city's informal settlements, also known as *favelas*. Militias provide apparently contradictory functions: they protect communities from violent state intrusion into the *favelas* by predatory and corrupt police, but they also dominate communities politically and socially through the use of violence and other forms of coercion.[63] In a context of increasing urbanisation, sustainable development cannot be promoted successfully in situations of chronic violence any more than in the context of more traditional armed conflict. To quote *The Report of the High-level Panel of Eminent Persons on the Post-2015 Development Agenda*: 'Cities are where the battle for sustainable development will be won or lost.'[64]

Business enterprises are not only affected by urbanisation, of course, but sometimes drive it. Company towns built around mills or mines have been part of the history of urbanisation on every continent. But in already complex environments, the emergence of a 'fragile city' can be part and parcel of the investment itself. 'The extraction of oil, gas, and strategic and precious metals is typically accompanied by a significant urbanization of the adjoining area, with often-dramatic socio-economic repercussions.'[65] And it is the smaller cities that can experience such pressures most intensely. Moramanga in Madagascar, for example, was completely transformed with the opening of a nickel and cobalt mine. Foreign workers and security personnel and labourers from other parts of Madagascar – including former members of the armed forces – changed the social and political dynamics of the town. After the mine opened, violence increased, especially armed break-ins and sexual and gender-based violence.[66] More generally, the intersection of mining and urbanisation has been found to increase conflict over the control of land and natural resources, and social unrest related to socio-economic and environmental conditions.[67] In many cases, citizens have no recourse to public authorities to regulate these conflicts as 'frontier urbanization' is 'rarely accompanied by sufficient public service provision, including security'.[68]

The effect of population pressures on conflict will be exacerbated by climate change. The International Panel on Climate Change finds with 'very high confidence' that 'impacts from recent climate related extremes, such as heat waves, droughts, floods, cyclones, and wildfires, reveal significant vulnerability and exposure of some ecosystems and many human systems to current climate variability'.[69] In some countries, the effects are already a present-day reality. São Paolo in Brazil is essentially dry,[70] and drought will become an ever more important feature in Mexico.[71] The US Department of Defense estimates that climate change will have wide-ranging security implications 'because it will aggravate existing problems ... that threaten domestic stability in a number of countries'.[72]

Increasingly, stresses on the environment also contribute to conflict. Globally, demand for food is expected to rise by at least 35% by 2030; demand for water is expected to rise by 40% in the same period.[73] These environmental pressures come at a time of unprecedented economic growth: British Petroleum forecasts a 41% increase in world energy demand from 2012 to 2035, with 95% of this coming from emerging economies.[74] The mismatch between need and availability of resources, as well as the overall pressure to find and exploit additional resources, creates new sources of conflict, even as it exacerbates old ones. In the Blue Nile State of Sudan, for example, the Rosario dam supplied irrigation to commercial farms and electricity to distant factories while local villages went without lights or running water. This was a factor in the renewed outbreak of violence in 2011 between government forces and local militias made up of people who felt excluded from any benefits of the activities around them.[75] Such examples underline that businesses may not only create conflict in the ways in which they operate – they may increasingly find themselves perceived as competitors for scarce resources such as energy and water.

It is not only climate and the environment that are undergoing change; the structure of politics is also shifting in ways that make conflict more likely. Over the last few decades, there has been a tremendous fragmentation of formal political authority. From the perspective of global governance between nation states, 'There are now almost four times as many states as there were in 1945. This increase in players makes international consensus harder to reach.'[76] Moreover, there has also been a proliferation of different types of actors. In 1945 there were only 41 non-governmental organisations (NGOs) with consultative status with the United Nations Economic and Social Council, the central forum for the discussion of international economic and social issues; this figure increased to 4,186 in 2014.[77] And since its founding in 2000, the United Nations Global Compact – a UN initiative to encourage global businesses to adopt sustainable and socially responsible policies – has grown to include more than 12,000 corporate participants and other stakeholders from over 145 countries.[78]

Beyond these trends of fragmentation, forecasts also suggest that there will be a growing diffusion of power: 'Enabled by communications technologies, power almost certainly will shift more toward multifaceted and amorphous networks composed of state and non-state actors that will form to influence global policies on various issues ... Networks will constrain policymakers because multiple players will be able to block policymakers' actions at numerous points.'[79] This trend is thought to be supported by the ever-growing reach of the internet.[80] These diffused sources of power and influence are also far less likely to be amenable to policy initiatives at the interstate level. One forecast suggests that 'If the international system becomes more fragmented and existing forms of cooperation are no longer seen as advantageous to many of the key global players, the potential for competition and conflict also will increase.'[81] Overall, these developments call for new perspectives and pragmatic responses to the changing strategic landscape of conflict and violence.

Business entanglement in conflict and violence

As outlined in Chapter One, there are companies that use violence to meet their objectives, or that profit from a conflict-prone environment, with gross indifference to the circumstances around them; these are the cases most directly addressed by international discourse around the predatory multinational company. The complex dynamics described above, however, suggest a far wider range of impacts of multinational companies on conflict and fragility. Many of these are unintentional from the perspective of company management, and yet are all the same highly problematic in a particular local environment.

Some impacts flow directly from a company's activities, for example, the resettlement of people to make way for a new dam or highway. While such impacts occur in developed as well as developing countries, in impoverished places, they may result in children needing to travel further to school, or in women working harder and longer to collect firewood. Families may end up destitute if they have difficulty re-establishing their livelihoods in a new location, whatever the level of compensation provided. While some will benefit from jobs or subcontracts, the presence of a new, large enterprise may drive local price inflation in the market and increase property and rental costs. This then leads to a decline in the standard of living for significant portions of the local population, particularly its already vulnerable segments. An influx of people seeking opportunities or a sudden increase in the amount of cash in the local economy can be accompanied by an increase in prostitution or alcohol abuse or changes in social structure within the community.[82] All of these represent significant stress factors in already fragile places.

Indirect impacts of company operations may exacerbate existing social tensions, for example, concerning political power and authority. At the national level, policy or regulation related to the company or its industry may fuel conflict over the relative authority and roles of the national parliament and the executive, particularly where these were already in question. In the case of Uganda, explored in greater detail in Chapter Four, this escalated to the point where the president effectively accused members of parliament of treason. At the local level, new people may, in light of dissatisfaction with a company's operations, step forward to represent the community, challenging existing patterns of legitimacy and representation; or traditional governance structures and authorities can be undermined when highly employable young men gain influence through unprecedented access to money and the ability to gain favours or respect. If not managed well, such disruptions may lead to competing power centres and other negative consequences that increase competition and conflict.

Often, a company's presence may force dormant conflicts to the surface. In Uganda, for example, land claims among neighbouring chiefdoms could remain contested over decades, without fuelling acute conflict. As soon as a decision had to be made as to which political authority would manage the company payments earmarked for local development, however, violent conflict erupted as the land claim now had resource and power implications.[83] Such land conflicts, which began with international investment in the oil sector from 2007, continue today.

Additionally, company operations implicate a variety of risk factors for violence, and thus affect physical security. In-migration from elsewhere in the country or region to the communities neighbouring a company's operations typically increases petty crimes affecting ordinary citizens and small local businesses. Changing levels and patterns of income can lead to increasing rates of domestic and gender-based violence. In one instance, people attributed the inability of their community to resist political violence to the loss of social cohesion they had experienced due to an influx of new people.[84]

At the same time as a large-scale investment directly or indirectly causes conflict, it many undermine a community's ability to cope with it. A defining feature of fragile environments is the lack of institutions with the legitimacy or capability to manage acute socio-political tensions, such as the accumulation of unfulfilled expectations and small grievances that create a growing sense of imbalance between winners and losers from an investment. Changes in income levels, status and patterns of interaction brought about by the company's presence and operations can disrupt the group identities and social relationships – between men and women, landowners and landless, different generations of people, or migrants and locals – upon which conflict prevention and resolution efforts greatly depend. Should company recruitment favour the employment of women in a garment factory or of young people in a high-technology repair facility, for example, this may alter family dynamics or inter-generational power relations. While such change is not always necessarily bad, it can damage mutual support networks and patterns of trust, undermining communities' resilience and allowing conflicts to fester.

These dynamics are exacerbated when companies establish new or parallel institutions – company grievance procedures that are unconnected to legitimate local institutions, for example – that weaken existing ones. In one case, a company wanting to provide water to a community sank a borehole at a location that was later discovered to be on private property owned by a Christian. Tensions escalated along religious lines as members of the community's Muslim majority felt that they had a right to access the water. When negotiations failed to settle the matter, the company assumed that local government should decide the issue. This led it to overlook a respected sheikh to whom both Muslims and Christians had traditionally gone to resolve disputes. The company's attempt to appeal to government authority bypassed the locally legitimate process for dealing with such conflicts, allowing the conflict to escalate unnecessarily into violence.[85]

Finally, companies may be caught up in conflicts not at all of their own making. These are often tied to legacies of the past. An agribusiness company may enter a market where prior industry players have played a particularly negative role in national politics; an industrial concern may be taking over from a state-owned factory with an abysmal environmental record; or an operating company in the extractives industry may be the fourth or fifth entity in a chain of exploration, development and production activities, along which any number of conflicts may have festered. Because communities see the new entrants as extensions of the old players, even a company that considers itself new to a fragile state market and which has not yet done anything to provoke conflict may find itself confronting tension and fear.[86]

Further complicating this landscape is a proliferation of corporate actors in fragile states that may not resemble their Organisation for Economic Co-operation and Development (OECD) counterparts in terms of environmental, social or labour policies and that are less subject to national or international control. These may include state-owned or multinational enterprises from the former Soviet Union, China, the Middle East or elsewhere in the Global South. Of the five largest greenfield foreign direct investment (FDI) projects announced in transition economies for 2014, only one came from a developed economy;[87] meanwhile, the net value of cross-border mergers and acquisitions sales in least developed countries (LDCs) rose to US$3.7bn in 2014 'on the back of acquisitions by Asian investors in African LDCs'.[88] These included the US$2.6bn acquisition by India's state-owned Oil and Natural Gas Corporation Limited of a 10% stake in an oil and gas exploration block in Mozambique, and banking acquisitions by Qatar National Bank, which has announced its intentions to become the largest bank in Africa and West Asia by 2017. In 2012, nine countries stood out in their LDC investments: Brazil, China, India, Malaysia, the Republic of Korea, South Africa, Thailand, the United Arab Emirates and Vietnam.[89] International policy-makers have apparently yet to fully digest the implications of this new landscape of international investment, continuing to focus primarily on Western multinationals within their reach.

Disconnect between international discourse and the strategic landscape

The complex dynamics of multinational companies within fragile state socio-political systems underline the fact that international actors must look far beyond the traditional focus on inter- and intra-state wars to address conflict and violence. To a limited extent, this has been recognised in emergent international policy and practice. The International Finance Corporation's Performance Standards on Environmental and Social Sustainability – a framework for environmental and social risk management – have adopted from international development practice the commitment to 'do no harm to people and the environment … to achieve positive development outcomes', and to ensure that 'the costs of economic development do not fall disproportionately on those who are poor or vulnerable'.[90] Its first performance standard, 'Assessment and management of environmental and social risks and impacts', now incorporates the 'due diligence' logic of the UN Guiding Principles on Business and Human Rights. The 'Respect' pillar of these Ruggie Principles requires 'A human rights due-diligence process to identify, prevent, mitigate and account for how they address their impacts on human rights'.[91] There is, however, a significant disconnect between these largely aspirational norms and standards, and experience on the ground.

While many point to a lack of willingness by international companies to respect these standards as the primary reason for this disconnect, perhaps a less obvious factor is the lack of corporate capabilities. Mary Anderson, an authority on outside intervention in conflict-prone environments, noted that 'peace is not an area for amateurs'.[92] For companies to effectively apply such principles, they must 'perform accurate and up-to-date conflict analysis; establish comfortable, trusting, and transparent relationships with diverse people who may not share their values; use specialized mediation skills to identify common concerns that can unite antagonists while also respecting fundamental differences and opposing positions; and have the ability to be calm and comfortable in situations of danger, threat, and emotional and physical stress'. In what is perhaps a pronounced understatement, she concludes that these 'are not common, everyday skills found among corporate managers'.[93] Anderson's comments echo studies suggesting that global companies require business competencies in areas in which most managers have no background or training, including the competencies needed to deal with foreign country interests, multiple domestic and foreign pressure groups, or international conflict.[94] Furthermore, attempts to outsource these functions result in a kind of corporate dyspraxia, in which companies fail to act effectively even on known risks to their own security or economic interests, due to governance and management systems failures.[95]

The more important disconnect between international policy and practice and business-related conflicts on the ground – including efforts to restrain predatory international companies, to promote private-sector investment for security and development, and the emerging discourse on 'due diligence' and 'do no harm' – may lie in the nature of international policy formation itself. Even as the landscape of business and conflict changes substantially, and the actors become more numerous and more diverse, international discourse and its policy expressions focus on agreement among actors at the international level, working to coordinate actions only among the most accessible and most willing players. The Ruggie Principles, for example, emerged from a diplomatic process focusing on states, multi-national companies primarily from countries belonging to the OECD, and international civil society. With Ruggie's work now having been taken over by the UN Human Rights Commission, the Principles' primary mechanism of implementation is through national action plans developed by the very fragile state governments whose failures to protect populations from human rights abuses created momentum for the development of the Principles in the first place.

Moreover, the disconnect between international policies and realities on the ground can mean that, even where companies intend to support them, the effects of implementing these policies can be perverse. For example, attempts by the UK food retailer Tesco to direct the development of a farm labour grievance mechanism pursuant to its understanding of its 'Ruggie' responsibilities were found to have undermined dialogue by local actors on the broader drivers of conflict and violence in their communities.[96] Similarly remote from local realities, initiatives such as the Extractives Industries Transparency Initiative (EITI) or Publish-What-You-Pay (both of which work in the area of transparency in the oil, gas and mining industries) are mainly involved in changing the reporting patterns of international companies with fragile state governments. But they have little reach to the dynamics of conflict over revenue sharing or resource allocations in a specific context. These and other international initiatives seem increasingly disconnected from the emerging landscape of highly localised and context-specific business and conflict in fragile states.

The lack of prioritisation of local drivers of conflict

Chapter Two concluded that the two dominant international discourses on business and conflict in fragile states unfold largely in parallel universes; they coexist but rarely intersect. What this chapter shows is that the narratives of the predatory multinational company and of business as a foundation for peaceful development share one critical characteristic: a focus on private enterprises as the crucial lever for resolving conflict in fragile states. These two dominant discourses take as their starting points distinct perspectives. In the former narrative, if businesses can be compelled to follow increasingly well-articulated and well-enforced rules and norms, then business-related conflict can be contained and managed. In the latter narrative, if business can be enabled and companies encouraged to take on ever greater leadership roles, the causes of conflict will be addressed. But whether working to restrain or unleash the multinational company, both narratives and their respective international policy responses largely locate the problem and the solution within the private sector.

While the proponents of each narrative may mainly talk past each other or argue with one another, from the outside one can see both approaches as attempts to use international financial, political and development policy levers to regulate corporate behaviour in fragile states. The unifying theory behind these international policy responses might therefore be described as, 'If we get the international incentives and disincentives for corporate behaviour right, then conflict related to large-scale business investments in fragile environments can be prevented or managed'. There is a determined focus on international levers for controlling fragile state conflict and violence through corporate action.

This perhaps makes most sense in the historical context from which both dominant discourses about business and conflict in fragile environments developed. The Bretton Woods institutions, which still hold enormous sway over economic policy towards fragile states, sought to address the perils of interstate conflict by creating a 'human welfare framing of international security' based on 'rights-based liberalism'[97] rooted in private enterprise. The Organisation for European Economic Co-operation (OEEC) was the predecessor to the OECD that today plays an influential role in international development policy towards fragile states through its Development Assistance Committee (DAC). The OEEC was established to manage the Marshall Plan for stabilising fragile European economies and keeping them out of the Soviet orbit as the Cold War unfolded.[98]

Those who would hold companies accountable for their misdeeds similarly find inspiration in the trials of corporate leaders for crimes against humanity at the Nuremberg military tribunals, themselves part of an international architecture to 'ensure freedom from fear of aggressive war'.[99] Organisations and institutions to some extent adapted to the world of intra-state conflict in the ensuing Cold War years – although even these were often enough characterised as proxy fights for the larger inter-state conflict between East and West.[100] But as inter-state and civil wars remained the major lens through which to gain an understanding of conflict and violence in fragile states in the post-Cold War era,[101] both dominant policy discourses towards business and conflict remain rooted in world views where national governments and international actors, for better or worse, control conflict dynamics, and therefore hold centre stage.

International discourse and policy have not adapted to the new realities of business and conflict in fragile states that fall outside the optic of inter- and intra-state conflict. Observations on the changing strategic landscape are not new: trends such as urbanisation, climate change, environmental degradation, and geopolitical tension and their probable impacts have been repeatedly highlighted in forecasts over the last three decades.[102] Indeed, these stresses may be reaching a certain 'tipping point' – 'that one dramatic moment when everything can change all at once'.[103] Perhaps this phenomenon has already occurred in North Africa and the Middle East; similar tipping points may be reached in fragile states in Central and South America, Asia and Africa sometime in the next decade as they experience ever-heightened tension as the new frontier markets for economic growth.

And yet, because of the uncertain timeline for diverse pressures to converge into crisis around business and conflict in fragile states, these developments may take on the characteristics of a so-called 'slow-onset emergency', one that does not 'emerge from a single, distinct event but one that emerges gradually over time, often based on a confluence of different events'.[104] Compared to acute crises, such slow-onset emergencies are particularly likely to be deprioritised by international actors.[105] International discourse and policy – whether to deter companies from promoting or profiting from conflict or violence, or to promote the private sector as the foundation for stability in so-called 'post-conflict' countries – thus remain stuck in the old world of interstate and intrastate wars. Policymakers deprioritise the more local, more complex and increasingly more prominent conflict dynamics in fragile states as they slowly but inexorably unfold.

The consequences of the deprioritisation of the changing landscape of conflict and violence, and thus of the local dimensions of business and conflict in fragile states, are twofold. Firstly, even if a company could and would respond perfectly to the incentive structure of international policy, it cannot, by itself, ensure reasonably stable or conflict-free operations. The changes brought about by the multinational corporation's activities in commercial agriculture, infrastructure development or the extractives industries are only a subset of the ameliorating or stress factors present in an already complex environment; its acts and omissions are intertwined with the full array of social, political, economic and conflict dynamics in a fragile setting. Furthermore, a variety of actors – from large-scale criminal enterprises to local army commanders to local youth gangs – will seek to bend the presence of the international company to their own purposes; as the managing director of an engineering services company based in a conflict-prone Latin American country noted, 'While the company is trying to shape the environment, you need to remember that other actors are trying to shape the company.'[106]

Secondly, local-level dynamics determine whether conflict and violence will be fomented or prevented, but international-level policy priorities will not in any predictable or dependable way address local stakeholders' priorities and perspectives. It is perhaps not contentious to observe that states that successfully emerge from fragility will generally be characterised by higher levels of per capita GDP, better infrastructure and better trading relationships with their neighbours than they exhibit today. International policy is, consequently, geared to promote these macroeconomic conditions. But, too often, a mining concession agreement is directed primarily at driving GDP growth and national government revenues at the expense of regional players, a particular infrastructure project moves forward on contested land, or an agricultural productivity initiative to create competitive exports puts a significant number of people out of work. Projects that are meant to help reduce fragility become significant drivers of conflict and violence at the local level. This is because the international policies that promote them do not meaningfully account for the interests of the range of local actors actually deciding whether or not there will be conflict and violence at a particular time in a particular place.

International policy outpaced by investment flows

As shown by the creation of the new China-led Asian Infrastructure Investment Bank, the pace of large-scale private investment in fragile states is accelerating, despite the conflict and violence that too frequently accompanies it. Developments are increasingly driven by local dynamics in fragile states – the need for energy in Ethiopia, for example, or indigenous desires for Africa to feed itself – and the new dynamics of emerging economies – for example, gold for India or iron ore for China.

Businesses, driven fundamentally by profit motives, are not necessarily deterred by the inherent conflict risk. A Multilateral Investment Guarantee Agency (MIGA) analysis of the gap between risk perception and investment behaviour noted that 'the potential for high returns over a short payback period is likely to convince some investors to operate in a high-risk environment'. Its 2010 survey of why political risk does not deter investment in conflicted-affected and fragile economies found two dominant factors across sectors, company size and geographical origin: (i) business opportunities outweighed risks; and (ii) potential losses were limited. In fact, fears of conflict and violence are not primary; 'Anticipation of the 1994 devaluation of the CFA franc in Côte d'Ivoire had a more severe negative impact on FDI flows than the eruption of political conflict toward the end of the 1990s, during the entire period of which it remained positive.'[107] Businesses will increasingly invest in fragile states despite the very real risks that their presence and operations will create and exacerbate conflict, and that they will be caught up in socio-political and socio-economic struggles. A sober analysis must admit that, at least today, the international policy regime of incentives and disincentives for business will do little to change this dynamic.

This analysis in no way intends to denigrate significant international efforts to address business and conflict in fragile states over the long term. International norms and standards influence thinking and action in both home and host countries of investment; an internationally led initiative like EITI, for example, can be successful in opening a window for activism at the local level.

The problem, rather, is the belief that these initiatives are central to resolving today's conflicts related to large-scale investments and those on the near horizon. Most businesses, the fragile state governments that seek to attract them and the local actors who decide to oppose them, are neither conflict-averse nor particularly responsive to the international policy regime meant to manage business and conflict. In short, current levels of fragile-state investment are already beyond the management capacity of international or host state institutions, and conflict and conflict potential are growing faster than current international policy and regulatory frameworks can hope to address.

Notes

[1] See Earthrights, 'The Yadana Pipeline', http://www.earthrights.org/campaigns/yadana-pipeline.

[2] Mary B. Anderson and Brian Ganson, *Report of the Fifth CDA/CEP Visit to the Yadana Pipeline in Myanmar/Burma* (Cambridge, MA: CDA, 2008).

[3] Burma Campaign UK, 'Halt All Dams Now in Salween River and All Ethnic Areas – Protests at Dam Sites', 14 March 2015, http://burmacampaign.org.uk/halt-all-dams-now-in-salween-river-and-all-ethnic-areas-protests-at-dam-sites.

[4] See http://www.myanmar-responsiblebusiness.org.

[5] Measured in terms of the extent of

forest. See Food and Agriculture Organization (FAO), 'Global Forest Resources Assessment' (Rome: FAO, 2010), p. 230.

6   Environmental Investigation Agency, 'Myanmar's Rosewood Crisis' (London: EIA, 2014).

7   World Wide Fund for Nature (WWF), *Ecosystems in the Greater Mekong: Past Trends, Current Status, Possible Futures* (Geneva: WWF, 2013).

8   Editorial Board, 'The Plunder of Myanmar', *New York Times*, 23 January 2015.

9   Atul Sethi, 'Buddhist–Rohingya Clashes: Economy the Real Trigger?', *Times of India*, 11 July 2013.

10 Alastair Leithead, 'Burmese "Slavery" Fishermen Are Trafficked And Abused', *BBC News*, 25 April 2015.

11 Timo Kivimäki and Paul Pasch, *The Dynamics of Conflict in the Multiethnic Union of Myanmar. PCIA Country Conflict-Analysis Study* (Berlin: FES, 2009).

12 Chetan Kumar, 'Building National Infrastructures for Peace: UN Assistance for Internally Negotiated Solutions to Violent Conflict', in Susan Allen Nan, Zacharia C. Mampilly and Andrea Bartoli (eds), *Peacemaking: From Practice to Theory* (Santa Barbara, CA: Praeger, 2011), p. 384. Based on United Nations Development Programme data.

13 ICRC, 'How is the Term "Armed Conflict" Defined in International Humanitarian Law?' ICRC Opinion Paper, 2008, p. 1, https://www.icrc.org/eng/resources/documents/article/other/armed-conflict-article-170308.htm.

14 History of the United Nations – 1942: The Declaration by United Nations, http://www.un.org/en/sections/history-united-nations-charter/1942-declaration-united-nations/index.html.

15 Preamble of the UN Charter, available at http://www.un.org/en/sections/un-charter/preamble/index.html.

16 Achim Wennmann (ed.), *20 Years of 'An Agenda for Peace': A New Vision for Conflict Prevention?* (Geneva: Geneva Peacebuilding Platform, 2012).

17 Peter Wallensteen, *Understanding Conflict Resolution* (London: Sage, 2007), pp. 16–22.

18 Martin Hollis, *The Philosophy of Social Science: An Introduction* (Cambridge: Cambridge University Press, 1994), pp. 40–51.

19 See the definition of the Uppsala Data Conflict Programme, http://www.pcr.uu.se/research/ucdp/definitions/definition of_armed_conflict.

20 Thérése Pettersson and Peter Wallensteen, 'Armed Conflict 1946–2014', *Journal of Peace Research*, vol. 52, no. 2, 2015, p. 536.

21 Paul Collier, Lani Elliott, Håvard Hegre, Anke Hoeffler, Marta Reynal-Querol and Nicholas Sambanis, *Breaking the Conflict Trap: Civil War and Development Policy* (Washington, DC: World Bank, 2003). For a critique, see Christopher Cramer, 'Homo Economicus Goes to War: Methodological Individualism, Rational Choice and the Political Economy of War', *World Development*, vol. 11, no. 11, 2002.

22 See United Nations General Assembly (UNGA), *Report of the Security Council: 1 August 2014–31*

July 2015, document A/70/2 (New York: United Nations, 2015), pp. 10, 12–28.

23 OCHA, *Global Humanitarian Overview 2016* (Geneva: OCHA, 2015), p. 12.

24 Chronic violence occurs 'where rates of violent death are at least twice the average for the country income category, where these levels are sustained for five years or more and where acts of violence not necessarily resulting in death are recorded at high levels across several socialization spaces, such as the household, the neighborhood, and the school, contributing to the further reproduction of violence over time': Jenny Pearce, 'Violence, Power and Participation: Building Citizenship in Contexts of Chronic Violence', IDS Working Paper 274 (Brighton: Institute of Development Studies, 2007), p. 7.

25 Andrew Tomlinson, 'Putting the Pieces Together: Towards a Unified Approach to Prevention at the United Nations', in Wennmann, *20 Years of 'An Agenda for Peace'*, p. 18.

26 Geneva Declaration Secretariat (GDS), *Global Burden of Armed Violence: Lethal Encounters* (Cambridge: Cambridge University Press, 2015), p. 51.

27 UNODC, *Global Study on Homicide* (Vienna: UNODC, 2013), p. 58. Ranking based on violent death rate per 100,000 population in 2012 or latest available year.

28 Comparison of GDS and Uppsala data for 2012 made by the authors. See http://www.genevadeclaration. org/measurability/global-burden-of-armed-violence/ gbav-2015/interactive-map-charts.html and https:// uppsalaconflictdataprogram. files.wordpress.com/2013/09/ armedconflicts_2012.jpg.

29 GDS, *Global Burden of Armed Violence*, p. 51.

30 Based on comparison between 32,685 terrorism victims in 2014 and 377,000 victims annually between 2007–12. See Institute of Economics and Peace (IEP), *Global Terrorism Index* (Sydney: IEP, 2015), p. 2; and GDS, *Global Burden of Armed Violence*, p. 51.

31 UNODC, *Global Study on Homicide* (Vienna: UNODC, 2013), p. 11.

32 GDS, *Global Burden of Armed Violence*, p. 87.

33 UNODC, *Global Study on Homicide*, p. 14.

34 World Health Organization (WHO), *Global Status Report on Violence Prevention* (Geneva: WHO, 2014), p. 2.

35 *Ibid.*

36 Patrick Corcoran, 'Mexico Survey Reveals Extent of Criminal Attacks on Businesses', *InsightCrime*, 12 June, 2015, https://mail.google.com/ mail/u/o/#search/insight+crime/14e 0b4306e87998a?compose=14e1a767 9b3ff9ad.

37 See Carl Boggs and Tom Pollard, *The Hollywood War Machine: U.S. Militarism and Popular Culture* (London: Routledge, 2016).

38 See Christopher Cramer, *Civil War is Not a Stupid Thing: Accounting for Violence in Developing Countries* (London: C. Hurst & Co., 2006), p. 4.

39 David Keen, 'A Rational Kind of Madness', *Oxford Development Studies*, vol. 25, no. 1, 1997, p. 68.

40 David Keen, *The Economic Functions of Violence in Civil Wars* (London: IISS, 1998), p. 12.

41 *Ibid.*

42 Azam Ahmed and Paulina Villegas, 'As Frustrations with Mexico's Government Mount, so do Lynchings', *New York Times*, 23 January 2016.

43 David Keen, 'Incentives and Disincentives for Violence', in Mats Berda and David Malone (eds), *Greed and Grievance: Economic Agendas in Civil Wars* (New York: International Peace Academy, 2000), p. 22.

44 Achim Wennmann, 'The Political Economy of Violent Conflict', in *The Armed Conflict Survey 2016* (London: IISS, 2016), pp. 19–32.

45 Stathis N. Kalyvas, *The Logic of Violence in Civil War* (Cambridge: Cambridge University Press, 2006); Patricia Justino, Tilman Brück and Philip Verwimp (eds), *A Micro-Level Perspective on the Dynamics of Conflict, Violence, and Development* (Oxford: Oxford University Press, 2014).

46 Organisation for Economic Co-operation and Development (OECD), *Think Local, Act Global: Confronting Factors That Influence Conflict and Fragility* (Paris: OECD, 2012).

47 Mary B. Anderson and Marshall Wallace, *Opting Out of War: Strategies to Prevent Violent Conflict* (Boulder, CO: Lynne Rienner, 2013).

48 Pettersson and Wallensteen, 'Armed Conflicts 1946–2014', pp. 536, 539.

49 This is, of course, a heated debate. See Steven Pinker, *The Better Angels of Nature: A History of Violence and Humanity* (London: Penguin, 2011); for a discussion of the 'declinist thesis' see Human Security Report Project, *Human Security Report 2013: The Decline in Global Violence: Evidence, Explanation, and Contestation* (Vancouver: Human Security Press, 2013), pp. 17–48.

50 Aske Nørby Bonde and Achim Wennmann, *Risks to Peace: A Review of Data Sources* (Geneva: Geneva Peacebuilding Platform, 2015).

51 Friedrich Glasl, *Confronting Conflict* (Bristol: Hawthorn Press, 1999).

52 Stated by Peter Maurer, 31 October 2015, available at https://www.icrc.org/en/document/peter-maurer-respect-laws-of-war.

53 See The Millennium Project (TMP), *2013–14 State of the Future* (Washington, DC: TMP, 2014), p. 42.

54 *Ibid.*

55 Michael Waithaka, Miriam Kyotalimye, Timothy S. Thomas, and Gerald C. Nelson, 'Summary and Conclusions', in Michael Waithaka, Gerald C. Nelson, Timothy S. Thomas, and Miriam Kyotalimye, (eds), 2013. *East African Agriculture and Climate Change: A Comprehensive Analysis* (Washington, DC: International Food Policy Research Institute, 2013), p. 378.

56 International Organization for Migration, '*Background Research on the Great Lakes Region*', unpublished.

57 Paul Richards and Jean Pierre Chauveau, *Land, Agricultural Change and Conflict in West Africa: Regional Issues from Sierra Leone, Liberia and Côte d'Ivoire* (Paris: OECD, 2007).

58 Malabo Declaration on Accelerated Agricultural Growth and Transformation for Shared Prosperity and Improved Livelihoods, p. 3, http://pages.au.int/sites/default/files/Malabo%20Declaration%202014_11%2026-.pdf.

59 *Ibid.*, p. 7.

60 United Nations Department for Social Affairs (UNDESA), *World Urbanization Prospects* (New York: UNDESA, 2014), p. 1.

61 WHO, *Urban Population Growth* (Geneva: Global Health Observatory, n.d.); Humansecurity-cities.org, *Human Security for an Urban Century: Local Challenges, Global Perspectives* (Ottawa: Canadian Consortium on Human Security, 2007), p. 9; Robert Muggah, *Researching the Urban Dilemma: Urbanization, Poverty and Violence* (Ottawa: IDRC, 2012), p. 1.

62 Oliver Jütersonke and Robert Muggah, 'Rethinking Stabilization and Humanitarian Action in "Fragile Cities"', in Ben Perrin (ed.), *Modern Warfare: Armed Groups, Private Militaries, Humanitarian Organizations, and the Law* (Vancouver: University of British Columbia Press, 2012), pp. 311–27.

63 Johanna Wheeler, 'Brazil: Citizenship, Violence, Power and Authority in Rio's favelas', in Alexander Ramsbotham and Achim Wennmann (eds), *Legitimacy and Peace Processes: From Coercion to Consent* (London: Conciliation Resources, 2014), pp. 86–9.

64 United Nations, *The Report of the High-Level Panel of Eminent Persons on the Post-2015 Development Agenda* (New York: United Nations, 2013), p. 17.

65 Oliver Jütersonke and Hannah Dönges, 'Digging for Trouble: Violence and Frontier Urbanization', in *Small Arms Survey 2015: Weapons and the World* (Cambridge: Cambridge University Press, 2015), p. 37.

66 *Ibid.*

67 *Ibid.*, p. 53.

68 *Ibid.*, p. 37.

69 The Core Writing Team, Rajendra K. Pachauri and Leo Meyer (eds), *Climate Change 2014: Synthesis Report* (Geneva: International Panel on Climate Change, 2014), p. 15.

70 Marussia Whately and Rebeca Lerer, 'Brazil Drought: Water Rationing Alone Won't Save São Paulo', *Guardian*, 11 February 2015.

71 Jonathan Amos, 'US "At Risk of Mega-drought Future"', BBC News, 13 February 2015.

72 US Department of Defense, *Response to Congressional Inquiry on National Security Implications of Climate-Related Risks and a Changing Climate*, 23 July 2015, p. 3, http://archive.defense.gov/pubs/150724-congressional-report-on-national-implications-of-climate-change.pdf?source=govdelivery.

73 National Intelligence Council (NIC), *Global Trends 2030: Alternative Worlds* (Washington, DC: NIC, 2012), p. v.

74 TMP, *2013–14 State of the Future*, p. 155.

75 Dost Bardouille-Crema, Diana Chigas and Benjamin Miller, 'How Do Our Operations Interact with the Environment?', in Brian Ganson (ed.), *Management in Complex Environments: Questions for Leaders* (Stockholm: International Council of Swedish Industry, 2013), p. 79.

76 Oxford Marten School Commission (OMSC), *Now for the Long Term* (Oxford: Oxford University Press, 2013), p. 18.

77 See http://csonet.org/.

78 See https://www.unglobalcompact.org/AboutTheGC/index.html.

79 NIC, *Global Trends 2030*, p. 19.

80 OMSC, *Now for the Long Term*, p. 23.

81 NIC, *Global Trends 2030*, p. 64.

82 Bardouille-Crema, Chigas, Miller, 'How Do Our Operations Interact with the Environment?'

83 Brian Ganson, *Risk and Risk Mitigation in the Oil and Gas Sector in Uganda* (Geneva: Geneva Peacebuilding Platform, 2012).

84 Bardouille-Crema, Chigas, Miller, 'How Do Our Operations Interact with the Environment?'

85 *Ibid.*

86 Paul Hollesen, 'Is Our Own House in Order?', in Ganson, *Management in Complex Environments*, p. 208.

87 UNCTAD, *World Investment Report 2013* (Geneva: UNCTAD, 2013), p. 65.

88 *Ibid.*, p. 80.

89 *Ibid.*, p. 74.

90 International Finance Corporation (IFC), 'IFC Sustainability Framework: Policy and Performance Standards on Environmental and Social Sustainability' (Washington: IFC, 2012), p. 8.

91 Office of the United Nations High Commissioner for Human Rights (OHCHR), 'Guiding Principles on Business and Human Rights: Implementing the United Nations "Protect, Respect and Remedy" Framework', HR/PUB/11/04 (Geneva: OHCHR, 2011), p. 16.

92 Mary B. Anderson, 'False Promises and Premises?', in Oliver F. Williams (ed.), *Peace Through Commerce* (Notre Dame, IN: University of Notre Dame Press, 2008), p. 125.

93 *Ibid.*, pp. 125–6.

94 Raymond Saner, Lichia Yiu and Mikael Søndergaard, 'Business Diplomacy Management: A Core Competency for Global Companies', *Academy of Management Executive*, vol. 14, no. 1, 2000, pp. 80–92.

95 Brian Ganson, 'Business in Fragile Environments: Capabilities for Conflict Prevention', *Negotiation and Conflict Management Research*, vol. 7, no. 2, 2014, pp. 121–39.

96 Hendrik Kotze, *Farmworker Grievances in the Western Cape, South Africa* (The Hague: ACCESS, 2014).

97 Elizabeth Borgwardt, *A New Deal for the World: America's Vision for Human Rights* (Cambridge, MA: Harvard University Press, 2005), pp. 134–135.

98 *Ibid.*, p. 119.

99 *Ibid.*, p. 204.

100 See, for instance, Janice Gross Stein, 'Proxy Wars – How Superpowers End Them: The Diplomacy of War Termination in the Middle East', *International Journal* vol. 35, no. 3, 1980, pp. 478–519.

101 See, for instance, Michael W. Doyle and Nicholas Sambanis, *Making War and Building Peace: United Nations Peace Operations* (Princeton, NJ: Princeton University Press, 2006).

102 Carla Koppell with Anita Sharma, *Preventing the Next Wave of Conflict: Understanding Non-Traditional Threats to Global Stability* (Washington, DC: Woodrow Wilson International Center for Scholars, 2003); Commission on Global Governance, *Our Global Neighbourhood* (Oxford: Oxford University Press, 1995); World Commission on Environment and Development, *Our Common Future* (Oxford: Oxford University Press, 1987).

103 Malcom Gladwell, *The Tipping Point: How Little Things Can Make a Big Difference* (New York: Back Bay Books, 2000), p. 9.

104 United Nations Office for the Coordination of Humanitarian Affairs (OCHA), *OCHA and Slow-Onset Emergencies* (New York: OCHA, 2011), p. 3.

105 Rob Bailey, *Managing Famine Risk: Linking Early Warning to Early Action* (London: Chatham House, 2013).

106 Interview by Brian Ganson with the regional manager for an engineering services company in Colombia.

107 MIGA, *Investment and Political Risk in Conflict-Affected and Fragile Economies* (Washington DC: MIGA, 2010).

CHAPTER FOUR

The limits of state-building

Since 1987, the Norwegian government has provided assistance to Angola – the second-largest oil producer in Africa after Nigeria – 'to improve the government's capabilities to develop, direct and control petroleum activity'. Aid is now consolidated under Norway's flagship Oil for Development programme, launched in 2005, which brings together Norway's Ministries of Foreign Affairs, Petroleum and Energy, Finance, and the Environment with its Agency for Development Cooperation. The programme in effect exports the country's 'decades of experience in the oil and gas sector', hoping to achieve 'economically, environmentally and socially responsible management of petroleum resources'[1] and to 'target poverty reduction'.[2] In Angola, this primarily means support for the government's planning, institutional capacity development, data management, and revision of laws and regulations.[3] These Norwegian efforts complement initiatives of other international actors, including International Monetary Fund (IMF) support for the establishment of a sovereign wealth fund (using Norway as a model) and legislation reform. Such efforts helped Angola to achieve 'solid economic growth, with single-digit inflation, a strong international reserves position, and a stable exchange rate ... The non-oil sector continues to grow strongly as investments in roads and power bolster growth in construction and manufacturing.'[4]

Yet this international investment in Angola's capacity to manage its economy has translated neither into conflict risk mitigation nor poverty reduction. It remains a country where 'many aspects of the war economy – slave labour, brutal treatment of poor people, weak regulation of lucrative activities – have carried over into a peacetime economy characterized by lip service to multi-party politics and market-oriented economic reform'.[5] Angola ranks 43rd out of 55 countries on the 2015 Ibrahim Index of African Governance, with some governance issues appearing 'to be slowing down, if not reversing', especially in terms of the business environment and accountability.[6] Ongoing socio-political conflict was highlighted by the November 2013 attack by government security forces on opposition parties' headquarters in order to suppress protests, resulting in multiple deaths.[7] This was just one example among many of authorities targeting activists with 'criminal defamation lawsuits, arbitrary arrests, unfair trials, intimidation, harassment, and surveillance', and responding with 'excessive force ... to stop peaceful anti-government protests and other gatherings'.[8] State-building has resulted in a stronger government that continues to rely on international assistance to help it become more adept at managing the resources it controls; so far, however, it has not succeeded in reducing conflict or enabling development.

To some extent the analysis of Chapter Three can be taken as a defence of the state-building approach underlying much of international policy and practice towards business and conflict in fragile environments. If the system of incentives and disincentives for companies to stop exploiting fragility, mitigate the stress factors they introduce into already complex environments and make positive contributions is to work, then it needs administration. And if international levers are too remote from the increasingly complex and intensely local context in which conflict and violence unfold, then national laws and institutions should work better – at least under the assumption that there is a functioning, liberal state encompassing a working and accountable bureaucracy, a monopoly over the legitimate use of violence and the capacity to deliver on basic services to individuals within the state's territory.[9] International assistance therefore focuses on the composition and structure of national government, and on the functions the state apparatus should perform.[10]

The evidence from Angola and elsewhere is strong, however, that international actors have limited capacity to affect the political cohesion at the heart of state-building, particularly around issues of land, livelihoods, money and power implicated by large-scale private investment. Even if such approaches may in the long term support positive change, they are not fast enough or deep enough to mitigate conflict and violence risks related to the large-scale business operations of today and tomorrow. In turn, conflict over investments – whether and how they proceed, who wins and who loses, and who decides – can undermine state-building efforts. State-building approaches to business and conflict can therefore reinforce rather than address state fragility, exacerbating rather than mitigating conflict and violence.

The conundrum of state-building for business and conflict

The challenges of business and conflict in fragile states require two questions to be answered. The first question asks what kind of action needs to be taken for business investment to support stability and development – for example, an investment policy designed for inclusive growth or institutional capacity-building for the country. It addresses the end state or desired outcomes of effective reform. The second question asks how those so inclined – whether they are within government, members of the broader society or those trying to support positive change from outside – can gain traction on these or other positive changes in a fragile environment despite complex conflict dynamics. It focuses on the political economy and the 'art of the possible' of broad-based reform – for example, finding politically palatable mechanisms for analysing, discussing and making decisions about the benefits and risks of business operations on a more inclusive basis. Current international state-building policy and practice focus on the first question with great rigour. International actors largely ignore the second question of how to implement desired changes despite the very dynamics of political fragmentation, mistrust, exclusion and grievance that make a context fragile in the first place. They underestimate the slow pace and significant challenges of state-building, particularly in the face of elite capture of government institutions and the formal economy.

There is no end of advice for post-conflict or otherwise fragile states as they seek to attract investment. The World Economic Forum (WEF) gathers perspectives from business, government and civil society on sound resource exploitation in conflict-affected countries, covering issues from awarding company contracts to institutional and regulatory frameworks to stimulating broader social and economic development from private-sector investments.[11] The United Nations Environment Programme (UNEP) underlines the need for natural resources to be 'properly governed and carefully managed' to support economic recovery, sustainable livelihoods and confidence building lest, 'when the benefits are not shared', conflict resume.[12] The International Development Association – the 'fund for the poorest' of the World Bank – notes that governments need to provide 'signals of a real break with the past – for example, ending the political or economic exclusion of marginalized groups, corruption, or human rights abuses – as well as mechanisms to "lock-in" these changes and show that they will not be reversed'.[13] These and a host of other good practice analyses provide a reasonably comprehensive laundry list of policy and governance reforms that would, if put into practice, in all likelihood reduce the risk of conflict related to large-scale private investments. Indeed, a state that wanted to implement such reforms, and was capable of doing so, could in no meaningful way be considered fragile.

Such advice is typically framed as a series of 'shoulds' directed towards fragile-state governments, and generally includes a number of common threads: such governments should be inclusive; they should act against corruption and cronyism; they should invest wisely for the future. The 53-page WEF guidance developed in the context of a conference in Myanmar, for example, manages to present policymakers with a total of 129 'shoulds'.[14] Counsel appears to be offered under the premise that country leaders are searching for a blueprint for what Western policymakers would characterise as responsible, transparent and inclusive management of large-scale business operations, and that once one has been presented, leaders will be willing and able to implement it.

In many fragile states, however, this premise is simply contrary to the facts. Angola, for example, has been described as a 'state without citizens'[15] – the governing elite continues to view the majority of the population, which remains impoverished and lacks access to the most basic of services, as dispensable or irrelevant.[16] In such contexts, international policymakers are in effect exhorting fragile states to stop being fragile by implementing sound liberal policies and practices.

The ruling party of Angola, however, is not seeking to emulate Norway. It, along with its counterparts in Rwanda, Ethiopia and Sudan, have been characterised as 'statist and illiberal', with violence borne of revolutionary roots playing a central role 'in their political praxis and vision'.[17] In Afghanistan, 'even after the United States and its coalition partners have provided hundreds of millions of dollars to create new infrastructure and capacity' – ranging from efforts to develop tenders and attract investors to building institutional and technical capacity at the Ministry of Mines and Petroleum – 'self-sustaining Afghan extractive industries still seem a very distant goal', and 'the $488 million U.S. government investment in efforts to develop Afghanistan's extractive industries could be wasted'.[18] In these and many other cases, national leaders lack the ability or the inclination to share power and implement liberal reforms in the face of real and imagined enemies.

Even in those fragile states where there is more of an intent to implement reforms that will improve the impact of business investment on development, the building of functioning and inclusive institutions is at best a slow and laborious process. President Ellen Johnson Sirleaf of Liberia – former head of the Governance Reform Commission set up after the second Liberian civil war and winner of the Nobel Peace Prize – has made attracting foreign investment the centrepiece of her plan to increase employment and grow the economy;[19] in this, she is strongly supported by the World Bank and other multilateral agencies.[20] Yet it is clear that Liberia is pushing large-scale investment at a much faster rate than its institutional capacity to manage it can develop. A 2013 report by auditors for the Liberia Extractive Industries Transparency Initiative found that, of 68 government contracts surveyed, only six were compliant with Liberian law. Violations ranged from lack of competitive bidding to issuance of private-use permits for community forest lands to illegal contract clauses.[21]

In Uganda, while the drilling of oil test wells was raising expectations, the allocation of communal land for industry purposes was exacerbating tensions and the hope of employment was causing migrants to pour into presumptive oil-producing areas, the new frameworks and institutions meant to manage oil development were still being debated before parliament. In 2012 the National Environment Management Authority frankly admitted that it lacked the resources to carry out its mandate; although many dozens of wells were being drilled from 2006 in remote and highly sensitive environmental areas, with communities complaining of noxious fumes and polluted water, the government had scheduled the Oil Spill Contingency Plan to be developed only from 2012, and the Environmental Monitoring Plan existed only on paper.[22] This lag between institutional need and implementation has a direct impact on both people and the environment, at the same time undermining the trust needed to mitigate and manage conflict.

Legal and policy reform is often the focus of international attention, in part because it represents a relatively definable, contained and measurable development project, and in part because it is of particular importance to international capital. For example, Norway's Oil for Development assistance often encompasses regulatory and institutional frameworks that align with Norwegian experience. Development agencies such as Germany's GIZ have assisted the African Union (AU) to adopt an Africa Mining Vision for 'transparent, equitable and optimal exploitation of mineral resources to underpin broad-based sustainable growth and socio-economic development';[23] various UN agencies participated in the promulgation of the AU's 'Land Policy in Africa: A Framework to Strengthen Land Rights, Enhance Productivity and Secure Livelihoods' that calls for 'inclusive and participatory' processes 'engendering broad grass roots endorsement'.[24] Now a variety of international actors work to support the implementation of legal frameworks at the national level that are based on these AU policies.[25] These and other legal and policy reform efforts represent attempts, in effect, to legislate an exit from conflict and fragility, based on a liberal understanding of law as 'a continually more efficacious social engineering'.[26]

These initiatives, however, appear to ignore the weight of evidence from the study of law and development – that policy and legislation imposed on a society is a weak lever for change in developing countries. In order to be effective, 'institutions and norms' formalised in new legislative frameworks must 'ratify and enforce underlying settlements regarding the uses, and limits, of wealth and power';[27] new laws do not, by themselves, create a new social consensus. It should therefore not be surprising that regulatory frameworks – whether set at the international diplomatic level or in national capitals – may have little purchase in the places where business and conflict play out. Indeed, where there are unresolved tensions – between national and regional authorities over the control of private-sector activities, as in Peru, between traditional and state authorities over the allocation of land, as in Uganda, or between those who promote and those who oppose a free-market capitalist system, as in India – laws become 'a weapon in social conflict', wielded by the powerful. Attempted legal reforms therefore 'generate and exacerbate conflicts rather than resolving or softening them'.[28]

Struggles to build a state capable of managing large-scale business operations and their related conflicts are congruent with broader state-building experience. 'The basic failure' of the state-building model in practice has been characterised as 'the widespread illusion that state capacity and public organisations can be built by policy prescription from outside or by policy dialogue ... State institutions in reality develop on the basis of pressures to respond to demand for governance, of pressures from below as well as from above.'[29] This underlines the fact that the formal trappings of government – ministry reporting lines and budget allocations, for example – are not the fundamental institutions organising society as experienced by people in fragile states. 'The state' is much broader than 'the government', including 'the informal rules, shared under-standings and rooted habits that shape political interaction and conduct, and that are at the heart of every political system'.[30] Studies of state-building in countries such as Afghanistan or Iraq have shown that a state model without linkages to context, political economy and people's experience of life can complicate war-to-peace transitions.[31] In Somalia, 'top-down' state-building has been found to clash with existing political orders in a way that has generated more opposition to than support for state-building, with the result that 'spoilers' frus-trate demands for structural change.[32] Internationally promoted efforts to 'improve' economic management can 'threaten the rent-creation that holds the society together and in many cases challenge the very logic on which the society is organised. Not surprisingly, the elite and many non-elites resist, sabotage, or subvert such reforms ...'[33] In the aggregate, attempts at state-building based on the export of an idealised liberal state model have little to show.[34]

Perverse impacts of liberal state-building on business and conflict

Beyond its track record of ineffectiveness, the state-building agenda often proves counterproductive to the goals of stability and development, particularly when it intersects with the entrenched commercial interests of a country's elite. Recent quantitative analysis of GDP growth patterns in Africa notes that fast-growing economies do not score particularly well on governance measures (although they score better than slow-growing ones). The accompanying qualitative analysis suggests that this may be because the governments of these fast-growing economies focused on governance and institutional changes geared towards attracting large flows of investment, rather than on broader-based governance reform. Such changes are therefore made 'without any fundamental political restructuring' and avoid addressing broader domestic concerns over the distribution of benefits and the legitimacy of government in the eyes of the population.[35] So, while institutional reforms under the banner of 'state-building' may lead to higher levels of foreign direct investment and thus top-line GDP growth, they do not address (and may in fact exacerbate) the underlying drivers of fragility.

This analysis is echoed in critiques of institutional and governance reform in the agricultural sector, such as the G8 New Alliance for Food Security and Nutrition. The New Alliance – a platform launched in 2012 by African heads of state and government, corporate leaders and G8 members – claims as a primary focus government policies 'that will facilitate responsible private investment in agriculture in support of smallholder farmers',[36] acting in particular 'to improve investment opportunities'.[37] Human rights and development advocates complain, however, that the initiative primarily aligns national policies with corporate interests, and that it 'entails huge gaps in terms of transparency, participation and accountability'.[38] Critics have highlighted, for example, government action plans supported by the New Alliance that focus on investments in export crops grown on large plantations that have no apparent connection to the interests of smallholder farmers or local food security. Olivier de Schutter, former UN special rapporteur on the right to food, adds that governments have been making promises to investors 'completely behind the screen', with 'no long-term view about the future of smallholder farmers' and without their participation.[39] By supporting the agendas of those already in power to increase and control rents from large-scale commercial agriculture or other business activities, state-building directed towards the areas of greatest interest of foreign investors may thus 'preserve in the end, rather than reform, neopatrimonialism'[40] and its attendant elite control over resources.

It has long been noted that even leaders of countries with no intention of bringing about the changes promoted by international institutions become adept at the 'development speak' of liberal reform.[41] They may enact relatively minor measures that act 'as short-term signals that ensure developing countries attain and retain external support and legitimacy'. But they are in fact acting on the 'incentive to masquerade as the transformational leader needed to facilitate institutional reforms' supported by international donors to 'further their own financial, political or administrative goals'.[42] At the same time, it is sometimes unclear whether international institutions are duped by their government counterparts or intentionally complicit in their actions. One report estimates that 3.4 million people around the globe – from Peru to Ethiopia to the Philippines – were physically or economically displaced without respect for their human rights as part of World Bank-funded projects between 2004 and 2013; up to 30% of projects funded by the Bank in that period were deemed likely to cause resettlement. This included US$50 billion invested from 2009 to 2013 in projects with the highest risk rating for 'irreversible or unprecedented' social or environmental impact.[43] Yet the Bank largely relied on promises from recipient governments to respect international guidelines to which they had agreed, with neither oversight nor enforcement mechanisms in place. A former lead specialist of the World Bank's social development department said that 'There was often no intent on the part of the governments to comply — and there was often no intent on the part of the bank's management to enforce.'[44]

Similarly, the *Fundo Soberano de Angola* (Angolan Sovereign Wealth Fund) stresses its 'commitment to Angola's social and economic development and capital preservation for its people',[45] and was called 'a huge signal of discipline' by an economist of the World Bank,[46] which had supported its establishment. Yet with the Angolan president appointing his son as head of the Fund and a business partner as asset manager, it is hard to believe that the Fund represents a meaningful shift in the country's economic regime towards more inclusive or peaceful development. As in many other fragile states, international state-building assistance helps to ensure that Angolan 'institutions enabling and protecting rents extraction' are 'protected and buttressed', while the Angolan government itself ensures that 'institutions of power and revenue sharing' are 'side-lined and impaired', leading to 'monopolization, elite predation, and usurpation'.[47] Some international programmes purport to guard against this dynamic by setting guidelines that limit engagement only to countries with demonstrated commitment to transparency, human rights and the rule of law; but the fact that Norway's Oil for Development programme persists in providing assistance to Sudan and Angola, for example, tends to contradict this claim.[48]

The gap is broad between the espoused purposes of liberal economic policy and institutions as supported by international state-building practice, and delivery on the promise of more inclusive development by national governments. In many places, this feeds growing disillusionment: 'When governments fail to deliver and there are allegations of corruption', concluded a study of conflict in the extractives industries, 'this increases the chances of populist movements or new governments calling for radical redistribution of wealth.'[49] Indeed, these dynamics fuel conflicts on all continents. Research documents more than 90 significant political protests that have taken place in the past decade in more than 40 African countries,[50] belying perceptions of populations 'too rural, too poor, and too trapped by tribalism to engage in popular, non-ethnic politics', and suggesting that the urban poor will be key drivers of political change.[51] In Nicaragua, former Contra and Sandinista enemies have united to stop the construction of the Grand Interoceanic Canal that would displace them from their land, saying 'We might go to war, not because we all want that, but because there may be no other option.'[52]

Importantly, these protests occur in countries characterised by democratic institutions as well as in non-democratic states; the liberal political system is not delivering sufficient trust, cohesion or political consensus to reduce conflict risks in fragile states. People on the ground appear to be responding to what the research is increasingly telling us: even autocratic rulers with no intention of sharing power over the economy know that liberal institutions 'bestow onto their leaders a façade of democracy that enables them to maintain international and domestic legitimacy needed in today's day and age'.[53] Indeed, in the absence of some underlying commitment to sharing power and access to resources, institutions of a liberal democracy 'do not lower overall repression levels, but instead enable autocrats to use repression in more targeted and less costly ways. Dictatorships with multiple parties and a legislature, for example, are more likely to use repression to target and punish specific opponents, but less likely to use it to indiscriminately restrict civil liberties. By increasing incentives to participate in the regime, these institutions provide dictators with an additional form of surgically-targeted political control.'[54] In fragile states, 'parties, legislatures, and elections' – typically supported by international state-building efforts – 'are enhancing the durability of autocracies'.[55]

Some international state-building aid that is tied to large-scale private investment attempts to address this democratic deficit. Norway, for example, has supported an Angolan non-governmental organisation (NGO) to monitor public spending on education, health and agriculture and to submit findings 'to the relevant parliamentary committees and ministries' as well as engage in other advocacy activities. This initiative can point to some signs of limited impact on government spending patterns.[56] But it can make no claim to addressing fundamental power dynamics or drivers of conflict.

Indeed, externally generated attempts to mimic democratic oversight arguably exacerbate rather than address conflict. In Uganda, international development organisations supported both the non-partisan Parliamentary Forum on Oil and Gas (PFOG) as well as the Civil Society Coalition for Oil in Uganda to advocate greater environmental and social safeguards, more robust financial oversight and more limited ministerial powers. The Democratic Governance Facility – a basket fund of eight international development partners – additionally funded public consultation processes to influence the institutional and regulatory framework.[57] In response, the ruling party used its control over individual members to keep parliament from significantly altering the executive branch's legislative proposals, largely ignoring community and civil society concerns. President Museveni accused members of parliament and NGOs of 'acting on behalf of foreign interests' to 'cripple and disorient the development of Uganda's oil sector' during an address to parliament in December 2012.[58] In April 2013 the ruling National Resistance Movement (NRM) party expelled four members of parliament for indiscipline, accusing two of them of belonging to the PFOG, which it said was 'opposed to the NRM position on oil'.[59] In 2014 the government renounced any civil society oversight of oil revenues earmarked for development priorities under the new public finance bill, and backpedalled on its commitments made in 2008 to join the Extractive Industries Transparency Initiative (EITI). The checks and balances of the liberal system, including political protests, are 'increasingly seen not as a basic form of democratic political action but rather as a threat that must be controlled'.[60]

Despite these perverse, widespread and increasingly well-documented results, 'there seems to be no viable alternative to some version of liberal peacebuilding' in contemporary international policy and practice.[61] This results in a myopic emphasis on the benefits of a liberal economy and the institutions to manage it without attention to the inherent conflict risks, particularly from abrupt changes and external shocks. In Nigeria, for example, figures published by the country's National Bureau of Statistics reveal that the country's unemployment rate rose from 14.6% in 2006 to 23.9% at the end of 2011. Despite pronounced GDP growth, the poverty rate rose from 54.7% in 2004 to 60.9% in 2010.[62] These developments were partly the consequence of Nigeria's entry into the World Trade Organization (WTO) in 1995, and partly of the government's 'guided deregulation' policy, which was greeted with approval by international institutions.[63] More open markets and increasing Chinese imports[64] triggered (among other impacts) the collapse of the textile sector, which had been Nigeria's largest manufacturing employer.[65] Textile mills had accounted for 25% of manufacturing jobs, had generated US$9bn in revenues, and had directly or indirectly supported 17.2m Nigerians.[66] But by 2003, direct employment in the textile industry had been more than halved from its 1995 levels.[67] In Kano State alone, there had been 31 enterprises employing 90,000 or more workers; by 2012, this had dropped to six enterprises employing 2,000,[68] echoing a national drop from 180 textile mills in the mid-1980s to 25 in 2009, operating at only 29% capacity.[69] While joblessness does not by itself cause radicalisation, unemployment is cited as a prime factor underpinning 'young people's vulnerability to recruitment and radicalization by extremist or terrorist groups' in northern Nigeria.[70] As was noted by the governor of Kano State, particularly hard hit by Boko Haram, 'A very poor man who is looking for something to eat can easily be recruited by the insurgents.'[71]

The WTO – which asserts that the first benefit it offers is that it 'helps to keep the peace'[72] – makes no mention of the disappearance of the textile sector or its broader social, political and economic impacts in its 2011 Nigeria Trade Policy Review.[73] Pointing to the trade provisions introduced to protect Nigeria's remaining industry, the US representative to the WTO responded to the 2011 report saying, 'We are concerned by Nigeria's apparent departure from the open and market-based approach to development that Nigeria had been following.'[74] The US apparently saw no link between the rapid imposition of the laws and institutions of the liberal economy and the rising menace of Nigerian extremists, already acknowledged at that time as a threat by the US government.[75] Yet the imposition of economic models, laws and institutions on societies in which there is no underlying consensus about their desirability, or appropriate mechanisms for their implementation, often 'tests these institutions and the societies that depend on them, sometimes to breaking point'.[76] As in the case of Nigeria, when 'fragile and conflict-affected states are assumed to be in desperate need of the benefits of a liberalised, integrated, free-market economy',[77] there can be tragic and far-reaching consequences.

Confronting a horizon of conflict for business in fragile states

States that emerge from fragility will exhibit greater legal and institutional capacity than they do today, including the ability to successfully regulate private-sector investment in ways that reduce harm, support stability and promote inclusive development. While this chapter illustrates many clumsy or misguided projects of international actors, the point is not the wholesale dismissal of state-building efforts. Rather, it is to make clear that even state-building projects that may pay off in the long term are not an answer to today's conflicts that are associated with large-scale business investments, nor those of tomorrow.

Internationally driven state-building approaches are simply not effective enough. This is in part attributable to a lack of contextual understanding. As a review of Norway's Oil for Development programme illustrated, distant actors focused primarily on technical, financial and economic objectives lack a sufficiently nuanced understanding of the political economy; they do not engage in sufficient analysis of the key actors and the beneficiaries or losers from different attempts at reform. They thereby generate insufficient insight on possibilities for modifying the 'major power/resource asymmetry between the state and rights-holder groups' for them to be able to design effective governance interventions.[78] Their ineffective interventions can create perverse consequences, reinforcing rather than addressing power imbalances at the root of fragility. Indeed, fragile-state elites benefit directly when international actors such as the Organisation for Economic Co-operation and Development (OECD) declare 'state building as the central objective'[79] and support 'ownership of development priorities by developing countries'.[80] International donors follow this logic to treat the 'government in power' and the 'state and society' as one and the same actor, only setting priorities with, and allocating resources through, state elites. This allows them to co-opt international aid to support their partisan goals, exacerbating domestic conflicts.

While international state-building efforts are often ineffective or worse, state-building pursued at the national level is too slow to address the business-related conflict and violence fragile states increasingly confront. Authentic state-building is 'an endogenous and locally driven process' in which the state evolves from new power relationships negotiated between the different actors that make up a country's social and political order.[81] Since 'the evolution of a state's relationship with society is at the heart of state-building',[82] new laws and institutions – if they are to address fragility – need to emerge from socio-political consensus over their purpose and goals. Thus, even at best, 'state-building is not a quick process',[83] and is predictably contentious.

Given the limitations of both international and national state-building efforts, large-scale business investments in fragile states are entering – and will for the foreseeable future remain within – environments of highly contested political space in which conflict over their operations and impact is the norm.

Businesses that put excessive trust in the formal structures of national government as promoted by international actors will be at particular risk. They may be susceptible to the perspectives of ruling elites that 'bureaucratic enclaves of excellence and huge infrastructure projects can qualitatively reconfigure domestic political-economic systems', failing to see that the government in power has convinced no more than 'a "substantial minority" of their population of the benefits and legitimacy of their rule'.[84] Lulled by international financing and political risk instruments that typically require certain understandings between the company, the government and international institutions, or by bilateral or multilateral investment treaties among recognised state actors, these businesses may also tend to believe that they need only follow the 'universal' norms and standards promoted by international actors and at least formally endorsed by fragile-state governments to steer clear of conflict risks.

However, as a mining-sector manager working in Mongolia noted, 'While a legal framework must be negotiated with the national government, it is important not to confuse that with the agreement required from directly affected communities and their leaders. You should assume that customary law takes over 15 kilometres outside the capital and act accordingly.'[85] This proved true for Newmont Mining which, due to local opposition, has no access to attributable reserves of 6.5m ounces of gold and around 1.7bn pounds of copper from its US$4.8bn Conga mine project in Peru; this is despite national government support for the project, declarations from the capital that communities 'unanimously' supported operations and assertions that the opposition leader was 'no longer relevant'.[86] In fact, local residents elected as regional governor the main opponent to the project, despite (and perhaps because of) his imprisonment on corruption charges by the national government.[87] Whether intentionally or unthinkingly supporting entrenched players, companies and their international backers can feed existing conflict dynamics related to struggles for power and legitimacy as they secure, and then act according to, legal permission to operate from national authorities.

The preceding analysis argues for greater attentiveness to local actors; but the question of local permission can also be fraught with conflict. In places where companies fail to engage with local stakeholders, those prejudiced by a company's presence or operations will simply see the business as the ally of the most powerful elements of the national government that has provided, for example, the land for agricultural development or the contract for dam construction, and act against it accordingly. On the other hand, in places where companies do attempt to engage locally, they may face pressure from the national authorities not to do so. In Suriname, for example, there is no framework for the legal recognition of land rights of indigenous peoples, despite an order by the Inter-American Court of Human Rights that the country must develop one.[88] And so extractives companies that seek to negotiate the terms of their engagement with local leaders find themselves facing claims from the state that it is the sole voice for the Surinamese people. In either case, the resulting conflict among stakeholders with different ideas about the appropriate distribution of power between the periphery and the centre should not be surprising.

At least in the near term, there appears to be no state-centric solution to address large-scale investments that predictably increase rather than decrease the stresses on fragile-state systems. Such environments will for the foreseeable future experience low levels of social cohesion; pressure will be felt particularly at the local level where, as Chapter Three illustrated, conflict and violence primarily reside. In the midst of an ongoing struggle to determine who sets the rules, the company is legally required to comply with international law; it is unable to operate beyond the power and authority of the national government that controls the broad parameters of its operations. Yet, in order to prevent and manage conflict on a day-to-day basis, the company is compelled to remain attentive to 'local law': the rules, permissions and understandings informally asserted by a variety of regional and local governmental agencies, traditional authorities, religious leaders, formal rebel commanders or others whose voices and opinions determine the extension or withdrawal of social support for a project, whatever the national structures may say. Operating according to different perspectives and interests, these local actors work to determine the (for the most part unwritten) rules and regimes governing business, often bringing them into conflict with national authorities, the company and with each other.

International focus related to such 'informal' power and authority is often on actors widely viewed as illegitimate, for example, 'warlords'. Some approaches to governance may, as seen in the Democratic Republic of the Congo and elsewhere, involve acknowledging the warlords' de facto governance power in order to conduct business at all, rationalising relationships with, and legitimising, unsavoury actors.[89] But even where the local power is morally less problematic, such as in the case of a regional or traditional authority, companies all the same become part of a contested local political system. Businesses influence inputs into political decision-making, namely who participates in, and makes, decisions affecting a local population. And they play a substantial role in outputs from it, such as whether political decisions have resulted in benefits that are broadly seen as fair and appropriate. This puts them at the heart of conflict over state-building. Tensions leading up to the Marikana massacre in South Africa, for example, are explained in part by contested control over the allocation of jobs and the condition of worker housing among the mining company, local government, traditional authorities, competing labour unions and 'a host of criminal and trafficking networks emerging from the unregulated space'.[90] In dealing with such thorny issues, companies cannot rely on any great level of international support; state fragility at the local level is not widely discussed or addressed in international state-building policy or practice.[91]

The need for a new lens on business and conflict in fragile states

This book has up until now made a number of arguments that are intended to be largely uncontentious, and consistent with the weight of a growing body of evidence that can only be selectively illustrated in this work.

Firstly, both the narrative of business as a cause of conflict and violence in fragile states and the narrative of a robust private sector as one foundation for peaceful development are well grounded in long experience. For better and for worse, the private sector is a major player in places experiencing pronounced levels of conflict and violence. If greater stability and inclusive development are to be achieved, and the lives and livelihoods of many millions of people in fragile states are to be improved, then the question of the role of the private sector, and how it should be regulated or promoted, must be answered.

Secondly, the international policy responses that flow from these narratives – as different as they are in world view – are remarkably similar in their reliance on laws and formal institutions. Those attempting to regulate the company work to gain consensus on an enforceable treaty on business and human rights in New York and Geneva; to construct a binding international mechanism for the regulation of building safety in Bangladesh; and to empower civil society representatives and human rights advocates to advance democratic processes through liberal government structures in Angola and Uganda. Those attempting to unleash the positive power of the private sector for their part convene international business, fragile-state governments and development partners to reduce barriers to investment and growth, while promoting the development of state institutions capable of managing the liberal economy from Myanmar to Liberia to Colombia. Both policy strands require significant governance capacity for their implementation.

Thirdly, we do not need to question the long-term wisdom of these contemporary international policy directions to acknowledge that their related projects have, on the whole, limited (and in many places no) impact on the broad range of conflicts related to large-scale investments in fragile states that are happening today, and the many more that will arrive with the growing wave of business investment in these complex environments. These policy levers are hard pressed to address a new face of conflict in fragile states that is more local and more multi-faceted than the inter- and intra-state conflicts of the past. And state-building is too long and laborious a process for those who claim to be concerned with the lives of this generation and the next to see it as a realistic solution.

If the primary goal is to reduce destructive conflict over private-sector activities today in ways that lay a foundation for peaceful development tomorrow, then more pragmatic thinking and immediate action are called for. Conflict risk mitigation, conflict management and conflict resolution will need to be addressed directly and on their own terms, not through the long and tumultuous processes of state-building and international regime formation.

Notes

[1] Norwegian Petroleum Directorate, 'The Oil for Development Programme', 7 July 2011, http://www.npd.no/en/Publications/Reports/Oil-for-development-2010/The-Oil-for-Development-programme.

[2] Norad Evaluation Department, *Facing the Resource Curse: Norway's Oil for Development Programme* (Oslo: Norad, 2012), p. x.

[3] Norwegian Petroleum Directorate, 'Angola Report', 4 July 2011, http:// www.npd.no/en/Publications/Reports/Oil-for-development-2010/OfD-projects-Core-countries/Angola.

[4] International Monetary Fund (IMF), *Angola: Second Post-Program Monitoring* (Washington, DC: IMF, 2014), p. 1.

[5] Christopher Cramer, 'Trajectories of Accumulation Through War and Peace', in Roland Paris and Timothy D. Sisk (eds), *The Dilemmas of Statebuilding: Confronting the*

Contradictions of Postwar Peace Operations (Abingdon: Routledge, 2009), p. 142.

6   Mo Ibrahim Foundation, *2015 Ibrahim Index of African Governance: Country Insights – Angola* (London: Mo Ibrahim Foundation, 2015), p. 4.

7   Jon Schubert, 'Angola: Violent Repression of Peaceful Protests Highlights Risks of Dos Santos Succession', *African Arguments*, 27 November 2013.

8   Human Rights Watch (HRW), *World Report 2015: Angola* (New York: HRW, 2015), p. 58.

9   Rolf Schwarz, 'Post-Conflict Peacebuilding: The Challenges of Security, Welfare and Protection', *Security Dialogue*, vol. 36, no. 4, 2005, pp. 429–46.

10 Achim Wennmann, *Grasping the Strengths of Fragile States: Aid Effectiveness between 'Top-down' and 'Bottom-up' Statebuilding*, CCDP Working Paper 6 (Geneva: The Graduate Institute, 2010), p. 16; David Chandler, *International Statebuilding: The Rise of Post-Liberal Governance* (Abingdon: Routledge, 2010), pp. 8–9.

11 Network of Global Agenda Councils, *Natural Riches? Perspectives on Responsible Natural Resource Management in Conflict-Affected Countries* (Geneva: World Economic Forum, 2013).

12 United Nations Environment Programme (UNEP), *From Conflict to Peacebuilding: The Role of Natural Resources and the Environment* (Geneva: UNEP, 2009), p. 19.

13 International Development Association (IDA), *IDA's Support to Fragile and Conflict-Affected States* (Washington, DC: IDA, 2013).

14 Network of Global Agenda Councils, *Natural Riches? Perspectives on Responsible Natural Resource Management in Conflict-Affected Countries* (Geneva: World Economic Forum, 2013).

15 Steve Commins, Alina Rocha Menocal, and Timothy Othieno, *States in Development: Testing the State Building Framework* (London: Overseas Development Institute, 2009), p. 140.

16 Steve Kibble, 'Angola: Can the Politics of Disorder Become the Politics of Democratisation and Development?', *Review of African Political Economy*, vol. 33, no. 109, 2006, p. 530.

17 Will Jones and Ricardo Soares de Oliveira, *Africa's Illiberal State-Builders* (Oxford: Refugees Studies Centre, 2013), p. 5.

18 Special Inspector General for Afghanistan Reconstruction (SIGAR), *Afghanistan's Mineral, Oil, and Gas Industries: Unless U.S. Agencies Act Soon to Sustain Investments Made, $488 Million in Funding is at Risk* (Washington, DC: SIGAR, 2015), p. 16.

19 President Sirleaf, 'Annual Message to the 53rd Legislature', 26 January 2015, reprinted in The Perspective, http://www.theperspective.org/2015/0127201503.php.

20 See IDA, IFC and MIGA, *Country Partnership Strategy for the Republic of Liberia for the Period FY13–FY17* (Washington, DC: World Bank, 2013).

21 Moore Stephens LLP, *Final Report for the LEITI Post Award Process Audit* (Monrovia: Liberia Extractive Industries Transparency Initiative, 2013).

22 Based on interviews conducted by Brian Ganson.

23 African Union, *Africa Mining Vision* (Addis Ababa: AU, 2009), p. v.

24 African Development Bank (AfDB), African Union (AU) and Economic Commission for Africa (ECA), *Land Policy in Africa: A Framework to Strengthen Land Rights, Enhance Productivity and Secure Livelihoods* (Addis Ababa: AU–ECA–AfDB Consortium, 2010), p. 23.

25 See African Minerals Development Centre (AMDC), *A Country Mining Vision Guidebook: Domesticating the Africa Mining Vision* (Addis Ababa: AMDC, 2014).

26 Roscoe Pound, *An Introduction to the Philosophy of Law* (New Haven: Yale University Press, 1942), p. 47.

27 Michael Johnston, *Syndromes of Corruption: Wealth, Power and Democracy* (Cambridge: Cambridge University Press, 2006), p. 22.

28 Austin T. Turk, 'Law as a Weapon in Social Conflict', *Social Conflict*, vol. 23, no. 3, 1976, p. 276.

29 Karl Wohlmuth, *Good Governance and Economic Development: New Foundations for Growth in Africa* (Bremen: Universität Bremen, 1998), p. 44.

30 Organisation for Economic Co-operation and Development (OECD), *Supporting Statebuilding in Situations of Conflict and Fragility: Policy Guidance* (Paris: OECD, 2011), p. 31.

31 Lucy Morgan Edwards, 'State-building in Afghanistan: A Case Showing the Limits?' *International Review of the Red Cross*, vol. 92, no. 880, 2010, pp. 1–25.

32 Mark Bradbury and Sally Healy, 'Introduction', in Mark Bradbury and Sally Healy (eds), *Whose Peace Is It Anyway? Connecting Somali and International Peacemaking* (London: Conciliation Resources, 2010), pp. 6–9.

33 Douglass C. North, John J. Wallis, Steven B. Webb, and Barry R. Weingast, *Limited Access Orders in the Developing World: A New Approach to the Problems of Development* (Washington, DC: World Bank, 2007), p. 5.

34 Volker Boege, Anne Brown, Kevin Clemens, and Aanne Nola, 'Building Peace and Political Community in Hybrid Political Orders', *International Peacekeeping*, vol. 16, no. 5, 2009, pp. 599–615.

35 Pierre Englebert and Gailyn Portelance, 'The Growth-Governance Paradox in Africa', *Africaplus*, 6 January 2015.

36 New Alliance for Food Security and Nutrition, *Progress Report 2013–2014* (Washington, DC: USAID, 2014), p. 8.

37 *Key Facts: The New Alliance for Food Security and Nutrition* (Washington, DC: USAID, 2012), p. 1.

38 Wolfgang Obenland, *Corporate Influence through the G8 New Alliance for Food Security and Nutrition in Africa* (Aachen, Berlin and Bonn: MISEREOR, Brot für die Welt and Global Policy Forum, 2014), p. 15.

39 See Claire Provost, Liz Ford and Mark Tran, 'G8 Alliance Condemned as New Wave of Colonialism in Africa', *Guardian*, 18 February 2014.

40 Englebert and Portelance, 'The Growth-Governance Paradox in Africa'.

41 Jean-François Bayart, 'Africa in the World: A History of Extraversion',

African Affairs, vol. 99, no. 395, 2000, p. 259.

42 Matt Andrews, *The Limits of Institutional Reform in Development: Changing Rules for Realistic Solutions* (Cambridge: Cambridge University Press, 2014), p. 104.

43 Sasha Chavkin, Ben Hallman, Michael Hudson, Cécile Schilis-Gallego and Shane Sifflett, *Evicted and Abandoned: How the World Bank Broke its Promise to Protect the Poor* (Washington, DC: International Consortium of Investigative Journalists and Huffington Post, 2015), http://www.icij.org/project/world-bank/how-world-bank-broke-its-promise-protect-poor.

44 *Ibid.*

45 Fundo Soberano de Angola, http://www.fundosoberano.ao/language/en.

46 Patrick McGroarty, 'Angola Wealth Fund is a Family Affair', *Wall Street Journal*, 26 February 2013.

47 Inge Amundsen, 'Drowning in Oil: Angola's Institutions and the "Resource Curse"', *Comparative Politics*, vol. 46, no. 2, 2014, pp. 169–89. Citations taken from online abstracts available at: http://www.ingentaconnect.com/content/cuny/cp/2014/00000046/00000002/art00004.

48 Global Witness, *Fuelling Mistrust: The Need for Transparency in Sudan's Oil Industry* (London: Global Witness, 2009).

49 Paul Stevens, Jaakko Kooroshy, Glada Lahn and Bernice Lee, *Conflict and Coexistence in the Extractive Industries* (London: Royal Institute of International Affairs, 2013), p. 93.

50 Adam Branch and Zachariah Mampilly, *Africa Uprising: Popular Protest and Political Change* (London: Zed Books, 2015).

51 Interview with Adam Branch and Zachariah Mampilly, *African Arguments*, 23 March 2015.

52 Nehemiah Stark, 'Nicaraguan Farmers Resist Grand Canal, the World's Largest Construction Project', *Guardian*, 4 April 2015.

53 Andrea Kendall-Taylor and Erica Frantz, 'Mimicking Democracy to Prolong Autocracies', *Washington Quarterly*, vol. 37, no. 4, 2015, p. 76.

54 *Ibid.*, p. 73.

55 *Ibid.*, p. 78.

56 Elling Tjonneland, *The Norwegian People's Aid, Oil and Development: A Review of Oil for the Common Good (2007–2011)* (Oslo: CMI, 2012), p. 5.

57 Brian Ganson, *Risk and Risk Mitigation in the Oil and Gas Sector in Uganda* (Geneva: Geneva Peacebuilding Platform, 2012).

58 'Museveni Lashes Civic Critics and Foreigners, Praises Oil Scientists', Oil in Uganda (14 Dec 2012). http://www.oilinuganda.org/features/civil-society/museveni-lashes-civic-critics-and-foreigners-praises-oil-scientists.html.

59 Yasiin Mugerwa, 'Repeat of History as NRM Expels "Rebel" MPs', *Daily Monitor* (Kampala), 16 April 2013, http://mobile.monitor.co.ug/News/Repeat-of-history-as-NRM-expels--rebel--MPs/-/691252/1749452/-/format/xhtml/-/83ws7c/-/index.html.

60 Interview with Adam Branch and Zachariah Mampilly, *African Arguments*.

61 Roland Paris, 'Saving Liberal Peacebuilding', in David J. Francis (ed.), *When War Ends: Building Peace*

in *Divided Communities* (Aldershot: Ashgate, 2012), p. 49.

62 CLEEN Foundation, *Youths, Radicalization and Affiliation with Insurgent Groups in Northern Nigeria* (Lagos: CLEEN Foundation, 2014), p. 99.

63 World Trade Organization (WTO), *Trade Policy Review: Federal Republic of Nigeria* (Wt/TPR/S/39, 1998), p. 1.

64 Keith Bradsher and Adam Nossiter, 'In Nigeria, Chinese Investment Comes With a Downside', *New York Times*, 5 December 2015.

65 Chris Nwachuku, 'Nigeria: 100 Textile Factories Closed after Country Joined WTO', *This Day*, 20 May 2005.

66 Iliya Kure, 'Former Nigeria Textile Workers Still Struggling', *Voice of America*, 13 December 2012.

67 Toye Olori, 'WTO-CANCUN: Liberalisation Hurts Nigeria's Textile Industry'. *Inter Press Service* (Lagos, 4 September 2003), http://www.ipsnews.net/2003/09/wto-cancun-liberalisation-hurts-nigerias-textile-industry/.

68 Centre for Research and Documentation (CRD), *The State of Kano Textile Industries and its Effect on the Nigerian Economy: A Study of the Kantin Kwari Market in Kano State* (Kano: CRD, 2012).

69 'Nigeria's Textile Industry on a Rebound?', *This Day Live*, 28 May 2013.

70 CLEEN Foundation, *Youths, Radicalization and Affiliation with Insurgent Groups in Northern Nigeria*, p. xi.

71 See Robyn Dixon, 'In Nigeria, Child Beggars are Easy Recruits for Boko Haram Extremists', *Los Angeles Times*, 17 August 2014.

72 WTO, *The 10 Benefits: Peace*, https://www.wto.org/english/thewto_e/whatis_e/10ben_e/10b01_e.htm.

73 Trade Policy Review Body, *Trade Policy Review Nigeria* (WT/TPR/S/247) (Geneva: WTO, 2011).

74 WTO Trade Policy Review of Nigeria, 'Statement of the US Representative', 28 June 2011, https://geneva.usmission.gov/2011/06/28/tpr-nigeria.

75 US House of Representatives Committee on Homeland Security Subcommittee on Counterterrorism and Intelligence, *Boko Haram: Emerging Threat to the U.S. Homeland*, 30 November 2011, http://homeland.house.gov/sites/homeland.house.gov/files/Boko%20Haram-%20Emerging%20Threat%20to%20the%20US%20Homeland.pdf.

76 *Ibid.*

77 Peter Middlebrook, 'Building a "Fragile Consensus": Liberalisation and State Fragility' (Paris: OECD, 2012), p. 14.

78 Tjonneland, *The Norwegian People's Aid, Oil and Development*, p. 5.

79 OECD, 'Principles for Fragile States and Situations', http://www.oecd.org/dacfragilestates/the10fragilestatesprinciples.htm.

80 OECD, *Fourth High Level Forum On Aid Effectiveness: Busan Partnership for Effective Development Co-operation* (Paris: OECD, 2011).

81 OECD, *Handbook on Contracting Out Government Functions and Services in Post-Conflict and Fragile Situations* (Paris: OECD, 2010), p. 9. See also Charles Tilly, *Coercion, Capital and European States, A.D. 990–1990* (Oxford: Blackwell, 1993).

82 OECD, *Supporting Statebuilding in Situations of Conflict and Fragility*, p. 11.

83 *Ibid.*, p. 60.

84 Jones and Soares de Oliveira, *Africa's Illiberal State-Builders*, p. 6.

85 Interview by Brian Ganson.

86 Alex Emery, 'Newmont's Minas Conga Project Could Restart in 2014, Government Says', *BN Americas*, 30 December 2013.

87 Cecelia Jamasmie, 'Peru's Main Opponent to Newmont's Conga Mine Wins Local Elections', *InfoMine*, 6 Oct 2014.

88 Viviane Weitzner, *Tipping the Power Balance: Making Free, Prior and Informed Consent Work* (Ottawa: The North-South Institute, 2011).

89 David Booth, *Development as a Collective Action Problem: Addressing the Real Challenges of African Governance* (London: ODI, 2012); Jean-Pierre O. de Sardan, *Researching the Practical Norms of Real Governance in Africa* (London: Overseas Development Institute, 2008).

90 Keith Breckenridge, 'Marikana and the Limits of Biopolitics: Themes in the Recent Scholarship of South African Mining', *Africa*, vol. 84, no. 1, 2014, p. 158.

91 Marjoke Oosterom, *Fragility at the Local Level: Challenges to Building Local State–Citizen Relations in Fragile Settings* (The Hague and Utrecht: Hivos and ICCO, 2009).

CHAPTER FIVE

Responses to conflict that work

In the late 2000s, gang violence and heavy-handed security measures in response to it made El Salvador the most violent country in the world;[1] by late 2011 and early 2012, it still had higher levels of violent death than most countries that were at war. Yet in April 2012, the *Mara Salvatrucha* and *Barrio 18* gangs agreed to a truce, addressing years of violence between them. The decision to hold a truce was first and foremost made by the gangs themselves. The older generation of gang leaders realised the damage they had done to society and wanted to end the violence. They were also tired of the social exclusion and stigmatisation that prevented any gang member from having a normal life, even if they wished to exit the gangs.[2] But the truce was also tactical, for the older leadership saw it as a means of reasserting control over the younger gang membership that had gained power and threatened gang cohesion. The truce thus enabled the older generation of leaders to discipline their ranks.[3]

The truce was also a deliberate choice by the government. Facing pressure from mass media, business and the US government, the administration of President Mauricio Funes had to demonstrate that it was in control of escalating violence and address a growing feeling of social anxiety.[4] Based on the government's own dismal performance in violence reduction through heavy-handed security strategies – known as *'mano dura'* – and the clear understanding that the fighting between *Mara Salvatrucha* and *Barrio 18* was the key driver of violence, the president and the defence minister, Munguía Payés, opened the political space for discreet engagement of senior gang members. This meant allowing two facilitators from El Salvador – one a Catholic bishop, one an ex-guerrilla commander and former congressman – access to high-security prisons, where the gang leaders were located, to explore the feasibility of violence reduction. A truce was reached within weeks. The gangs themselves then delivered results to show that they were serious: for example, there was an immediate reduction in the homicide rate of more than 60%.[5] Overall, the truce lasted for two years.

Different actors played different roles in this home-grown process, in which many players 'were prepared to risk thinking "outside the box"'.[6] The government maintained a strategic distance from the truce negotiations because of their political sensitivity; great parts of the population, especially the middle classes and elites, were opposed to it because, in their view, negotiating with 'criminals' was both immoral and illegal. International actors did not directly intervene in the process, but provided targeted support as the truce developed that helped to maintain momentum over two years. The Organization of American States (OAS) acted as a guarantor of the peacebuilding process, the International Committee of the Red Cross (ICRC) established a special mission to monitor human rights conditions in El Salvador's prisons, and an international non-governmental organisation (NGO) provided discreet advice and technical support to the two facilitators. And from the corporate side, a group of business people established the Humanitarian Foundation to generate opportunities for jobs and encourage social integration of gang members.

El Salvador is far from unique. Local actors in many conflict-prone and fragile environments take the lead in resolving conflict through similarly deliberate and carefully tailored processes. The Colombian city of Medellín achieved a 90% drop in violence from 1991 to 2006 by means of a holistic strategy that would implement pacification and community policing, improve access by marginalised communities to basic services, change the built environment and spatial segregation of the city, create jobs for at-risk youth, promote social cohesion within the city, and improve urban governance for security.[7] Colombia has since developed more than 200 of such integrated initiatives, and Brazil has at least as many.[8] Despite the raging war in Syria, local communities negotiated at least 35 local ceasefires between 2011 and 2014.[9] In Somalia, at least 100 local processes over the last 20 years have managed violence and protected the cattle trade on which many livelihoods depend.[10] And, as illustrated by El Salvador, positive outcomes can often be achieved within surprisingly short time frames.

Just as importantly, conflict management and violence reduction efforts succeed despite conditions such as weak institutions, a lack of trust in government, legacies of past grievances and the presence of spoilers content to exploit conflict to meet their narrowly defined interests. These processes are far from perfect; in the case of El Salvador, spoilers exploited deep public divisions around the truce process. They undermined the truce, leading the country back into violence.[11] Yet what El Salvador and other cases all the same show is that success can be achieved by combining an understanding of the entire conflict system – defined by the particular social, political and economic dynamics among a specific set of actors in a certain time and place – with a pragmatic focus on the available levers of action on those issues that are most important.

These approaches are well enough established in the realms of peacebuilding, conflict prevention and violence reduction to broadly be considered mainstream. They are underpinned by reasonably well-understood principles and mechanisms of action. Furthermore, the available evidence from emerging business practice suggests that these solutions – based on granular analysis, the engagement of progressively broader coalitions for change, and iterative, well-monitored actions – can be equally well applied to prevent and manage conflicts in the context of large-scale business investments.

Getting a grip on conflict and violence

Effective conflict management builds first and foremost from a precise analysis and understanding of local conflict dynamics. A major research programme on the micro-dynamics of conflict, violence and development, funded by the European Commission, underlines the essentially local nature of violence:

> The outbreak, the continuation, the end, and the consequences of violent conflict are closely inter-related with how people behave, make choices, and interact with their immediate surroundings, and how all these factors may shape the lives and livelihoods of those exposed to conflict and violence.[12]

This work, consistent with a large body of research, underlines the fact that individuals, households, local groups and communities are central to an understanding of conflict dynamics.[13] Without such a granular and localised understanding of a conflict context, efforts at conflict reduction – particularly those of outsiders such as foreign investors, governments or development agencies – will almost inevitably be misdirected. In the Democratic Republic of the Congo (DRC), for instance, international action was premised on a war resulting from 'an international confrontation between the Congo and Rwanda, and an ethnic conflict that pitted indigenous Congolese against ethnic Hutus and Tutsis with Rwandan ancestry living in the Congo'.[14] Local understanding of the armed conflict, however, emphasised 'the primacy of land and other micro-level issues in causing violence and producing anguish, and the unspeakable horrors perpetrated on the Congolese population'.[15] It is not surprising, then, that an international intervention that took responsibility only for macro-level conflicts, and which precluded action on local conflicts, was ineffective in preventing major atrocities in the eastern DRC.[16]

In contrast, between 2009 and 2012, the Crime and Risk Mapping Analysis (CRMA) programme in South Sudan mapped 1,500 villages and collected more than 10,000 data points, becoming the most systematic data collection and mapping effort in any conflict-affected or fragile country. Through its mapping programme, it was able to identify areas of high need for malaria prevention efforts and priority areas for school infrastructure programmes, and also informed conflict prevention around community competition for access to water.[17] At the local level, the city of Diadema in Brazil reduced violence levels by around 44% from 2002 to 2004 after careful study of local patterns of violence, which among other insights revealed that 65% of murders were alcohol related. The city did so by combining controls on alcohol and gun sales, initiatives for non-violent conflict resolution, and public education programmes on crime and violence prevention.[18] Interventions that seek to understand and prioritise local dimensions of conflict appear, in general, to have a much higher chance of effectiveness.

Yet making sense of the local context and conflict dynamics is challenging in rumour-rich and information-poor environments. This is in part because data generation does not occur in a political vacuum; controlling information is an expression of political power that in turn favours or disfavours different interest groups. The above-mentioned CRMA programme in South Sudan initially faced substantial opposition from local officials because they feared the political consequences of transparency. The programme overcame this challenge by separating the data collection and data analysis from each other. International actors led on the data collection and systematisation – the largely technical exercise – while local actors took the lead on the data analysis. This provided political support for the continuation of data collection as decision-makers recognised its value to them, as well as time for local political dynamics to adapt to a more structured discussion of data and evidence.[19]

Additionally, stakeholders in fragile environments will often not trust information that they have not themselves had a hand in collecting, due to legacies of mistrust. In the Espinar Province of Peru, for example, sometimes-violent conflict continues between the company operating the Tintaya copper mine, the government and surrounding communities over long-standing allegations that the mine caused heavy metal pollution of soil and water in the area. After decades of broken promises by mine and government officials, animal- and human-health monitoring programmes – carried out first by company consultants and later by government institutions – failed to reassure neighbouring farmers. Local organisations took legal action against the Peruvian government, asking the court to order the government to declare an environmental emergency and to have independent epidemiology and toxicology studies carried out in the affected area.[20]

Finally, despite the availability of many different kinds of conflict analysis tools for local and international actors,[21] context and conflict analysis is generally not a core business process for companies, international organisations and other actors that need to make sense of a conflict-prone environment. Analyses typically remain incomplete, are carried out as a one-off exercise and are disconnected from policymaking.[22]

Increasingly, conflict management practice is overcoming these interrelated barriers to insight and analysis in complex and dynamic environments through the use of institutionalised mechanisms or networks for monitoring the local context. Often called 'observatories', they function to generate data, provide analysis or give advice to decision-makers to strengthen policymaking.[23] Their primary role is to help all actors to broaden their perspectives and confront the realities of their environment. This has a technical aspect, for instance, through the application of more rigorous qualitative and quantitative methods. But, as in the CRMA programme in South Sudan, the observatories also serve a political function. Events or seminars on data gathering or analysis organised by an observatory may be the first opportunity for actors from diverse sectors and perspectives to challenge each other's thinking. Moderated conversations uncover gaps in information and understanding, potentially faulty assumptions regarding cause and effect, and biases in both data collection and data reporting. Repeating such interactions over time allows stakeholders to collectively test assumptions underlying decision-making processes and strategies.[24]

Taking collaborative approaches to data gathering and analysis to the next level, an increasingly well-developed body of practice has grown up around community-based monitoring systems (CBMS). A typical CBMS trains local researchers to collect data at a level of detail and precision difficult to match by outsider-driven assessments; in the social arena, for example, it is not uncommon for a CBMS to collect data on every household in its defined area. Such approaches have been found to increase the validity, reliability, accuracy and legitimacy of data through its collection by those closest to it. It may also achieve real cost savings through the deployment of lower-cost local resources. And it can reduce disputes over data and analysis as different actors with a stake in a conflict and its resolution understand the assessments that underlie them.[25]

As a result of their practical and political value, observatories are widely used in Latin America: there are at least 95 in Mexico, 33 in Colombia, 26 in Argentina, 21 in Brazil and more than 270 in the whole region.[26] One of the most ambitious is a private sector-led initiative, the Operations Centre of the city of Rio de Janeiro. Designed by IBM at the request of Rio's mayor, the Operations Centre is a city-wide system that integrates data from some 30 agencies, all under a single roof.[27] Part of IBM's 'Smarter Cities Initiatives', the Operations Centre capitalises on new technologies and insights to transform city systems, operations and service delivery. It builds on the idea that city leaders can maximise transformative possibilities by using big data and analytics for deeper insights and better policies.[28]

Adopting these conflict management principles, credible local processes and institutions that build a common understanding of local conflict dynamics and their root causes are, in a variety of contexts, helping to manage business and conflict in fragile states. In the sugar cane town of Chichigalpa, Nicaragua, for example, one rallying point for chronic conflict was the belief that the environmental and working conditions at Nicaragua Sugar Estates Ltd were causing the chronic kidney disease (CKD) that was killing local residents, with about 200 new cases and 100 deaths in 2011 alone. In response to a complaint, the Compliance Advisor Ombudsman (CAO) of the World Bank Group convened a dialogue between one victim group and the company. The CAO assembled a multi-disciplinary team of professionals in hydrology, public health, mediation, business and human rights under expert facilitation, setting with the parties the agreed goal of 'determining and addressing the causes of [CKD]'. While the subsequent studies were funded by the CAO and the National Board of Sugar Producers of Nicaragua, they had credibility with community advocates who had been part of choosing the international research institution to carry out the work. The investigators remained in regular contact with the dialogue table, both keeping participants up to date with the scientific process and following their instructions about what to prioritise. As the mediator noted, 'The scientific process and the dialogue process were in this way one and the same.' While the complex socio-political issues of an impoverished and politically marginalised community are far from resolved, 'The process was able to address some of the immediate needs of the community, open new channels of communication and set the stage for continuing efforts to address CKD in the long term.'[29]

Approaches to collaborative data collection and analysis also work on a more systemic level in environments plagued by chronic conflict. The Chevron-supported Niger Delta Partnership Initiative (NDPI), for example, funds with other international donors the Partners for Peace (P4P) network. One of its core projects is the P4P peacebuilding map, which 'compiles the shared knowledge of the wider peace building community on the holistic patterns of conflict risk and the locations of peace building actors working to address those risk factors in the region'.[30] A 2014 review of the NDPI's work underlined the availability of such 'data and analysis to drive project decision making, not only during the design phase of projects but throughout their life cycle' as 'critical to producing sustainable results'.[31]

The rallying of diverse and sometimes conflicting local stakeholders around higher-quality data and more trustworthy analysis often lays the foundation for a further step in conflict prevention and conflict resolution practice, namely, the building of sufficient consensus for action. In practice, this means progressively enlarging the circle of actors aligned around a concrete vision for the future, ensuring that it be consensual, that it be as broadly owned as possible, and there be no major gap between the vision and the capacities of local or international stakeholders to deliver that vision.[32]

For example, a starting point for the move from conflict to greater stability in turbulent countries is often in the form of national dialogue processes, which are 'negotiating mechanisms intended to expand participation in political transitions beyond the political and military elites. Their ambition is to move away from elite-level deal making by allowing diverse interests to influence the transitional negotiations.'[33] Recognising that transitional mechanisms must be put in place to compensate for those of the formal government that lack sufficient legitimacy, they nurture 'a shared understanding among key political actors on principles'.[34] Their success rests at least in part on rigorous stakeholder mapping (which can be supported by the observatory function), as well as on an expanded understanding of 'who counts' in efforts towards stability and peaceful development. The importance of national dialogue processes was explicitly recognised in the awarding of the 2015 Nobel Peace Prize to the Tunisian National Dialogue Quartet 'for its decisive contribution to the building of a pluralistic democracy in Tunisia'.[35]

Explicit consideration of the political economy of conflict and its resolution leads towards a perspective that any party with a stake in the outcome – be it commercial, political or simply in raising the children of the town in peace – must somehow be included in the process of building consensus around new political institutions and a new course of action. This can make for large numbers of participants: in Afghanistan, the Loya Jirga (or grand council) of June 2012 included 1,051 participants; the 2004 Iraq National Conference had at least 648 participants.[36] Thankfully, not every interested party needs to be directly at the table; research drawing on the insights of more than 100 senior peace mediators suggests that a variety of options for inclusion are available. These range from direct representation or observation in negotiations, to consultative forums run in parallel to negotiations, to informal outreach to key stakeholders, to inclusive post-agreement mechanisms, to public participation through media events, town-hall or mass meetings, or information campaigns.[37] As a major study on legitimacy and peace processes that reviewed 12 specific cases concluded, what is critical for a process to be legitimate is popular consent – that is, that social and political agreements be accepted in the broadest possible way.[38]

Successful efforts to manage conflict related to business operations in fragile states often demonstrate analogous efforts to expand the circle of social support. A key lesson is that under-inclusive agreements foster conflict. As noted by the World Bank's 2003 Extractive Industries Review, 'Many grievances from communities and especially from indigenous peoples living near extractive industries projects relate to their claims that their rights to participate in, influence, and share control over development initiatives, decisions, and resources are ignored'.[39] At the national level, a company may out of commercial expediency seek only the accord of the national government, which in turn, to bolster its own status, may claim to speak for all the people. This leads both to complaints of immoral elite pacts,[40] and to conflict that undermines commercial and political goals. Palm oil companies in Liberia, for example, at one point brought into production less than 10% of the land area they had promised to the government and investors, largely because a failure to include affected communities in decision-making led to protests and operational disruptions.[41] Participation in decision-making at the local level also runs the risk of being too narrowly defined. Companies exploiting mineral or timber resources may work only with the most proximate communities, discounting the interests of affected communities along access roads or downstream waterways. Governments, conceptualising company–community engagement as 'private' agreements, may ignore their own role in managing public goods and absent themselves from discussions. As in the case of the Tintaya copper mine in Peru, disruptive and sometimes violent conflict results.[42]

Structured and deliberate efforts towards greater inclusion, in contrast, enable a path to less conflict-prone commercial development. To manage a legacy of mistrust between an open-pit mining company and a variety of neighbouring communities in the Philippines, the official delegates to a company–community roundtable included extra 'observers' to ensure transparency and proper representation of community interests. After consultations, 'the Community Relations Officers would walk back to the communities together with the representatives. Meetings were held, negotiation terms were recounted, and every party could be sure that they were being properly represented.' A senior mediator concluded: 'It is not just about trust among individuals, but also about confidence in the process.'[43] In Papua New Guinea, one company achieved the relatively smooth construction of a 700-kilometre pipeline affecting 100 communities through a culturally appropriate process that included social mapping and landowner identification, followed by extensive public consultation. The public information campaign included the provision of illustrated posters explaining the environmental impact of the pipeline, and the promotion of road safety through drama groups. These activities took place before and throughout the pipe-line construction process. A commentator close to the process noted that, in addition to reducing conflict risks, 'such efforts to promote clear communication and look at situations together … pay off in faster implementation down the line'.[44]

Such companies are apparently learning the lesson that disputes arising from investments and operations are not only about substantive issues such as land or water use, distribution of benefits, pollution or health and safety. Rather, at their heart is a struggle for control over the future vision for the community and the resources to implement it. A study comparing the experiences of communities affected by the operation of three different oil companies in the Niger Delta underlines the particular importance of this concept for companies operating in violence-prone areas. It found a clear relationship between the quality of engagement with local communities and their inclusion in decision-making, and the incidence of kidnap-pings, killings and protracted conflict at the local level.[45]

Data-gathering and analysis functions performed by obser-vatories can also underpin proactive conflict prevention and resolution interventions, which prove particularly impor-tant to conflict management practice. As noted one country manager of a mining company in Africa, 'Fragile contexts don't take surprises well. Reactions are much stronger. There is no button to press to calm down an angry population that feels betrayed.'[46] Systems capable of preventing the escala-tion of conflict or violence may take a variety of innovative forms. In Kenya, a group of technologists and civic activists built the Ushahidi platform in 2008 in response to election violence, allowing the public to report eyewitness accounts in real time and enable swifter responses. The platform has since been deployed in hundreds of different contexts around the world to support early warning. Recognising that 'calls to violent action spread faster over mobile phones and the internet', local groups in Kenya counter violence using these same tools. For example, the PeaceTXT programme of the NGO *Sisi Ni Amani* uses community informants who report as instigations to violence spread, triggering a targeted SMS with a positive message to people in high-risk areas that interrupts conflict escalation.[47] In other parts of the world, similar projects that incorporate crowd-sourced reporting on violence abound. Additionally, a new strand of early warning systems integrates 'big data' feeds – whether from social media or from digital media repositories such as GDELT[48] – to gather opinions and concerns that are not directly solicited.[49]

But effective conflict prevention can be decidedly low-tech as well. Increasing numbers of initiatives draw inspiration from the insight of public health experts, who have noted that violence spreads like a disease, and that it is therefore amenable to strategic interruption points. Programmes deploy trusted members of a local community – from ex-drug runners or gang leaders to religious figures or elders – as 'violence interrupters'. These community members are trained to intervene in crises, mediate disputes between individuals and intercede in group disputes to prevent violent events.[50] The role of interrupters in detecting and defusing conflicts, identifying and treating the highest-risk individuals and changing social norms is well documented in evaluations showing a measurable reduction in violence due to interrupter programmes.[51] The rich experience of peace mediation similarly underlines the value of 'insider mediators' – leaders of civil society organisations, churches, trade unions or business councils who leverage trust, respect and deep knowledge of the dynamics and context of the conflict in conjunction with a high level of legitimacy that is rooted in their social position, personality and skills. The fact that local leaders acting as mediators are connected to, and trusted by, important local constituencies has been found to build trust in processes and outcomes where the state is too weak or illegitimate to do so, de-escalating and managing conflict risks.[52]

Such thinking is being echoed in company approaches to proactive conflict intervention as corporate leaders broaden their field of vision from 'safe operations' – protecting their own people and assets – to 'safe communities' – a focus on the full range of conflict drivers in the socio-political context of which they are a part. As noted by an executive of a company with operations in multiple fragile contexts, this shift is driven by a hard-won understanding that the company cannot through its own actions alone protect its operational continuity or social licence to operate:

> The mere scale of company operations amplifies problems around it. And there are also conflicts between groups in society, in which conflict with the company is simply collateral damage. This puts the company in the business of reconciliation.[53]

As it committed an additional US$40 million in 2014 to the NDPI Foundation, Chevron as one example of this thinking explicitly linked its business success to 'peaceful co-existence in regions where we operate'.[54] As noted in Chapter Two, it organises its community relations under General Memoranda of Understanding (GMUs) with eight regional development councils, each of which represents a cluster of communities. Every council has a project review committee to identify, develop and implement community development projects; an accounts and audit committee to ensure transparency; and a peacebuilding committee. Through NDPI, Chevron further

supports P4P initiatives that 'focus on engaging and empow-
ering local actors in peace and conflict mitigation', explicitly
contrasting 'the traditional donor-driven, top-down approach
to peacebuilding implementation' with their 'local efforts that
address the salient conflict risk factors'.[55] These approaches,
taken together, have 'given community stakeholders a larger
role in setting the terms of the conversation, and the process
for interacting'. They provide a 'greater sense of fairness' that
'creates some of the key conditions for productive interaction
and problem solving'. Evaluations in 2008 and 2011 document key stakeholders' perceptions that, compared to the
pre-2003 period before GMUs were introduced, Chevron's
new approaches notably contributed to a 'dramatic' reduction
in violence, both against company operations and facilities,
and amongst communities that had formerly seen themselves
as pitted against one another.[56]

These interdependent facets of peacebuilding and conflict
management systems – improving conflict-related data and
analysis, providing platforms on which to convene diverse
stakeholders and build sufficient consensus for action, and
intervening to prevent or de-escalate acute conflict risks – will
often require professional and institutionalised support to coordinate and sustain them. Ad hoc processes convened directly
by stakeholders can die from the exhaustion of planning and
managing complex collaborative initiatives that are outside the
core mandate or expertise of any participant; as stated by the
G20 High Level Panel on Infrastructure, partnerships that bring
diverse actors together 'require their own infrastructure'.[57] Ad
hoc processes may also fall prey to wrangling among the players
as one or another is perceived to be manipulating the process
to achieve its preferred outcome. In the resolution of conflict
in particular, companies may face resistance from aggrieved
parties until they 'relinquish some measure of control over

decision-making'.[58] This is because communities must believe that their consent is 'enduring, enforceable, and meaningful' before they move 'out of their current defensive positions'.[59] This also argues for independent institutional support.

Whether under the rubric of 'mediation support' or another name, neutral assistance provides important expertise and plays a variety of vital roles. United Nations guidance on effective mediation suggests that, in situations of conflict, it may be necessary to help build relationships of confidence where they do not sufficiently exist among local actors themselves; to facilitate across a variety of actors the participatory analysis of conflict dynamics as well as local strengths and challenges faced in dealing with them; to ensure the careful evaluation of strategic and tactical options for introducing new thinking and new modes of action for conflict prevention into the fragile environment; to provide expert support for the design, management and evaluation of conflict prevention systems; and to engage in consistent outreach to the full range of stakeholders nationally and internationally for coherent action.[60] A 'backbone support organization' that provides services such as neutral facilitation or mediation, technology and communication, data collection and reporting, and administrative support is therefore increasingly seen as a critical enabler of complex collaborative efforts.[61]

An example of such an institutionalised approach to understanding conflict drivers and acting to prevent conflict escalation can be found in Ghana. There, local Peace Councils operate within a national legislative and institutional framework. They provide a mandate to, and support for, individuals widely considered as eminent personalities in their mediation of local conflicts ranging from land, labour or chieftaincy disputes to differences between and within political parties, backed up with an analysis of the root causes of conflict and capacity building at local and national levels.[62] The government of Ghana considers its system important in ensuring that the development benefits arising from the country's oil resources do not dissipate through political instability or armed violence.[63] Studies of business-centred conflicts confirm the value to both companies and communities of such institutionalised, safe places for dialogue and dispute resolution.[64]

When strategically combined, these deceptively simple building blocks of conflict management and peacebuilding practice – trustworthy data, collaborative analysis, progressively expanded coalitions for change, targeted interventions that address the most acute risk factors of conflict and violence, and sustained institutional support by an honest broker – have proven remarkably effective in preventing or de-escalating conflict in a wide range of settings. One key success factor appears to be the relentless focus on the reduction of conflict and violence that follows from these combined approaches. In Colombia in the mid-1990s, for example, the mayors of Medellín and Bogotá represented new political coalitions for anti-violence with a degree of political independence from traditional parties. A broad coalition across left and right, the media and a large part of the business community enabled policies for solving critical problems to take priority over the partisan interests of certain economic elites or municipal bureaucracies. In Cali, by contrast, traditional party politics and competing partisan interests limited violence reduction efforts.[65]

Prioritisation appears to enable another key success factor of conflict and violence reduction, namely the building of will and capacity for integrated approaches. In the Dominican Republic, for example, a programme to address crime and drug trafficking in the Capotillo neighbourhood of Santo Domingo in 2005 simultaneously increased the number of patrols by specially trained police in high-crime areas; provided new street lighting and new public recreational areas; invested in young people by providing new classrooms in schools, cultural workshops and sports clinics; and reached out to the general public with literacy and civic education initiatives. The programme recorded an 85% decline in assaults and robberies during its first two months, and a 70% reduction in homicides over eight months.[66] Chevron's simultaneous attentiveness to social, political, economic and conflict dynamics in the Niger Delta, described above, demonstrates that these principles of prioritisation and of diverse yet coordinated efforts can be equally well applied to prevent and manage conflicts in the context of large-scale business operations.

Making positive change despite fragility

The approaches to managing conflict and violence in fragile states surveyed above succeed in the face of social division, legacies of grievance, weak institutions, lack of trust in government, pressing socio-economic challenges, or the presence of spoilers content to exploit or tolerate conflict to meet their narrowly defined interests – that is to say, the very conditions that define fragility and enable conflict to fester and turn violent in the first place. As critiqued in the preceding chapters, the dominant contemporary international responses to business and conflict in fragile states may fail either because they assume away fragility – proffering advice which there is no willingness or political capacity to implement, for example – or because they assume they must prioritise giving fragile states the look and feel of their less fragile counterparts – for example, by imposing regulatory or institutional reforms even in the absence of an underlying socio-political consensus for their implementation. The broad evidence of peacebuilding and conflict management practice, however, is that successful approaches acknowledge fragility, working around, and even where possible with, prevailing socio-political dynamics to reduce the risk of conflict and violence.

Successful initiatives in fragile states begin by engaging parties on the basis of their partisan interests. In Kenya, for example, the business community remained peripheral to efforts to contain election violence until it became apparent that brutal and widespread conflict impacted its members, as businesses, directly. In 2008, one year after the contested elections, conflict had contributed to a 24% reduction in flower exports and at least a 40% decline in tourism, costing the tourism industry alone at least US$270m in lost revenue and more than 140,000 lost jobs. Export losses from the tea industry amounted to US$2m per day, and tea estates became a deliberate target of post-election violence.[67] Consequently, in the run-up to the elections in 2013, fraught with similar tensions, the business community made an affirmative choice to contribute to conflict prevention initiatives.

Local communities also make choices between conflict and peace based on partisan perceptions. A major study on local strategies for opting out of violent conflict found a rational calculation taking place, even among those who 'had fought in other wars'. People would 'fight if they felt a war were justified', yet would opt out if 'they simply calculated that the present war made no sense to them'.[68] Pointedly, many actors do not engage in conflict prevention efforts because they have an agenda for peace, but because conflict interferes with their more important priorities. Ethnic Georgians displaced from Abkhazia, for example, were often the marchers seen on Georgian television demanding harsh action against the breakaway province, presenting a particular barrier to peace efforts. A peacebuilding organisation engaged these internally displaced persons (IDPs) not around their attitudes towards the conflict with Abkhazia, but around their rights as Georgian citizens being undermined by a Georgian government seeking to manipulate them. A highly visible and activist IDP network thus emerged around an agenda for economic development and political inclusion. IDPs, coming to understand that their progress against these priorities was undermined by nationalist sabre-rattling, became a force that countered the more bellicose voices of the Abkhazia government-in-exile that had purported to speak on their behalf.[69]

In the context of business and conflict in fragile states, a rallying point may be that all role players face risks to their own agendas from conflict and violence. These may jeopardise a government's revenue and development plans; a company's operational continuity and reputation; civil society's agenda for good governance and human rights; and, most directly, the health, security and sustainable economic opportunity of local communities. As much as these parties may see themselves in opposition to each other on important issues, or fail to agree on a single vision for peaceful development, they share common interests in the effective management of conflict risks that may undermine the achievement of their own desired goals. Thus it was possible to rally and organise business, government and civil society actors in Kenya in collaborative initiatives to ensure the relative peacefulness of the 2013 election. These actors constituted more than 130 district peace committees that played an important role in conflict early warning and preventive action,[70] even as critical political divides between them persisted.

Party interests related to conflict and its management play out differently at the various levels of a fragile socio-political system. It is therefore often necessary to create vertical linkages – that is, relationships and channels of communication between different levels – in order to manage manifestations of conflict that present locally but can only be managed at a regional, national or international level. When a local councillor belonging to the African National Congress (ANC) political party was implicated in fomenting xenophobic violence for partisan political purposes in the Breede River Municipality of South Africa, for example, the local mediator convinced national ANC leaders to intervene to contain the local politician, leveraging the political party's interest at the national level in maintaining control over party structures.[71] Similarly, land contested by neighbouring communities may reflect at the same time a reluctance of the state to address indigenous claims going back to a colonial era; government policy to set aside wetlands or nature reserves without sufficient regard to the impact on local populations; land grabs by politically powerful individuals; and company failures to allocate royalties on a 'pooled' – shared among all community members in the area in which oil is found – rather than a 'wellhead' – paid only to the party owning the land on which the well is drilled – basis. Such conflicts cannot be fully resolved locally, but rather need action at different levels and across sectors.

A variety of approaches to institutionalising such vertical linkages are often described as 'infrastructures for peace'.[72] While these approaches predominantly work at the local level, they have connections and operating arrangements at the municipal, provincial or national level. Their main objective is to promote mutual understanding, build trust, solve problems and prevent violence.[73] Positive examples include the National Reconciliation Commission in Nicaragua and the Policing Board in Northern Ireland. At each level of the system, representatives 'from within the conflict settings who as individuals enjoy the trust and confidence of one side in the conflict but who as a team provide balance and equity' analyse conflict risk factors and agree on strategies for intervention.[74]

These infrastructures for peace often draw inspiration from the experience of South Africa's National Peace Secretariat, established to supervise the implementation of the 1991 Peace Accord. The national secretariat established 11 regional and more than 260 local peace committees, uniting representatives from political organisations, trade unions, business, churches, police and security forces, allowing issues to be managed locally if possible but also enabling them to be quickly escalated to another level of influence if necessary. The secretariat is considered 'a major breakthrough that helped to create the space for parties to engage in negotiations to decide the political future of South Africa'.[75] Echoing these approaches, the NDPI builds from its local peace and development structures to convene forums annually in the US, Nigeria and the UK 'to build common understanding of the complex security and economic challenges facing the people of the Niger Delta'.[76] In doing so, it enables coordinated action across local, national and international levels.

Successfully managing conflict and violence amidst fragility also requires recognition of the existing social and political capital from which effective efforts can be built. A typical international intervention may begin with a gap analysis, leading to the familiar litany in descriptions of fragile states of corrupt governments, divided communities and failed institutions. Yet the absence of functioning government institutions should not be mistaken for the absence of governance mechanisms or public service delivery, especially at sub-national levels. In a rural area where there are no state courts, justice may be delivered through a chieftaincy system that has endured for centuries. In an urban township where the police are unwilling or unable to act, neighbourhood committees may chase down suspects, try them in informal courts and mete out punishment. Even in the most difficult places, networks of trust and obligation help to ensure that informal taxi drivers keep their vans on the road and that bustling commercial centres thrive in the middle of 'failed' states. These locally legitimate structures and institutions, although different from the formal state towards which development agencies and companies are typically oriented, all the same represent 'a different and genuine political order'[77] from which conflict prevention efforts can build.

Finding and nurturing local capacities for conflict prevention requires looking past stereotypes in fragile environments to where real interests and capacities may lie. In Sierra Leone, for example, the Bo Bike Riders' Association is a motorcycle taxi cooperative made up of thousands of young men who for the most part previously belonged to one of the world's most brutal insurgencies, the Revolutionary United Front. Ex-combatants are at a high risk of returning to violence, and are often counted among those perceived to welcome conflict as a tool to pursue money, power, revenge or self-aggrandisement – and thus as difficult or impossible to engage. Yet the Bike Riders' Association was a critical partner in the 2007 Campaign for Violence-Free Elections, using its members' ubiquitous presence across the region to raise the alarm when violence threatened and, having defined itself as 'a peaceful, non-political organization', to 'move into the community to resolve conflicts and prevent violence'.[78] The Bo bike riders described their interventions with activists thus: 'They treated us as human beings. They confided in us and we confided in them.' Providing skills for 'advocacy, conflict transformation, and leadership' helped young men who 'had been waiting for revenge' to make a commitment to 'staying away from conflict' and 'helping one another', 'keeping hope of not returning to arms'. Through careful assessment of, and then appeals to, members' civic instincts, the well-regulated structures of the Bo

Bike Riders' Association could be activated for conflict prevention even in an environment where politicians 'gave money, drugs and alcohol' to youth to promote election violence.[79]

Local government may also represent a potential force for conflict prevention, as local governance capacity may be latent rather than entirely absent. In the Dominican Republic, for example, mining company Barrick Gold managed conflict reasonably successfully in the planning stages of its operations. The company recognised that there was a national legal framework for decentralisation and the development of municipal governance, but at the time of the company's intervention this legislative vision existed mainly on paper and not in reality. Rather than creating its own processes for community relations, Barrick supported local efforts to increase civic engagement and enable an increasingly capable local government to identify and address potential disputes.[80] In Peru, progressive companies that lent support both to the Peruvian Ombudsman's Office and to the creation of a mediation commission within the Ministry of Energy and Mines reduced their own burden of conflict management.[81] These experiences emphasise that 'many of the systems, institutions, attitudes, values, and interests that support conflict prevention are already in place' in conflict-prone environments,[82] and that such existing capacities can provide the foundation for meaningful progress.[83]

Finally, many actors in fragile environments are not necessarily indisposed to outside intervention, particularly when it comes in the form of expertise and advice rather than a pre-packaged plan or solution. In the Philippines, an International Contact Group, comprising both foreign government and international NGOs, supported the peace processes between the government and the Moro Islamic Liberation Front (MILF). Among other services, they provided technical inputs such as meeting design and resources for the parties to draw on in developing framework agreements, and engaged with a wide range of actors to explore new ideas.[84] In the negotiations on wealth sharing between Sudan and South Sudan from 2003–2004, the process benefited from the parties' participation in a crash course on oil economics to detail the intricacies of managing the contracts that were already in place between Sudan and oil companies, and the workings of oil markets.[85] Many parties are increasingly unwilling to tolerate peacebuilding efforts directed by external interveners, yet they may at the same time be open to accepting such limited but influential roles of external actors who accompany rather than direct them in their efforts to resolve conflict.[86]

Facilitating learning from one conflict context to another may be one such role of particular importance. In many circumstances, parties fall hostage to their own beliefs that conflict and violence are inevitable.[87] They become

> unable to communicate with each other, unable to think of a solution that could be attractive to the other side as well as themselves, unable to conceive any side payments or enticements to turn the zero-sum conflict into a positive-sum solution, and unable to turn from commitment and a winning mentality to problem solving and solutions to grievances.[88]

In such cases, outside intervention can help to address the narrowed perspectives and broken relationships underpinning fragility, as when South African experience was able to inspire the participants in the Northern Ireland peace process to break through deadlocks. Additionally, offering only advice and experience that the parties themselves will filter and apply in light of their superior understanding of local dynamics helps to protect against the all-too-common failure of international interventions that are disconnected from local social and politi-cal realities.[89] The findings of a multi-stakeholder process on conflict prevention in the context of large-scale business invest-ments suggest the need for a 'strategic focal point to facilitate international accompaniment of local efforts' in keeping with these principles.[90] This focal point would, in essence, collect and curate evidence on business-related conflict and its reso-lution, and deploy dedicated experts and facilitators to aid parties engaged in specific local efforts.

Local approaches to conflict and violence that mitigate fragility

As in previous chapters, there is no claim to comprehensiveness in the above inventory of conflict management, violence reduc-tion and peacebuilding practice, or the evidence supporting it. Rather, the chapter illustrates that destructive conflict and violence are neither inevitable nor unmanageable in fragile states, particularly at the largely local level at which interna-tional business operates.

Positive results emerge from addressing conflict risk mitiga-tion, conflict management and conflict resolution deliberately and on their own terms: the most promising armed violence reduction and prevention (AVRP) programmes are those that 'bring together a range of violence prevention and reduction strategies across a number of sectors and purposefully target the key risk factors' of conflict and violence, and that 'integrate AVRP objectives and actions into regional, national, and sub-national development plans and programmes'.[91] Successful management of business and conflict requires rigorous and sustained engagement in fragile states: in an increas-ingly complex landscape of local conflict, 'potentially violent tensions or on-going violence are increasingly insusceptible' to one-time intervention.[92] Positive results also emerge from stepping outside the formal state-building paradigm, reaching out to atypical actors, and building systems and institutions on the foundations of those functioning parts of society that are found in even the most fragile contexts.[93]

Furthermore, there is a rich toolbox of now-mainstream methods that can help to prevent and manage conflict risk at the local level in the context of large-scale business operations in fragile environments. These approaches to data collection, collaborative analysis, articulation of joint visions for positive change, interruption of conflict escalation, and monitoring and evaluation for continual adaptation are based on reasonably well-articulated principles and mechanisms of action. As illustrated in the many examples of this chapter, they can therefore be tailored by businesses, communities and governments to the constraints and opportunities of their particular environment to reduce risk factors for conflict and violence, as well as to manage those conflicts that will inevitably emerge. Doing so increases the likelihood both that business projects move forward and that peaceful development takes place.

The focus of this work has been the management of business and conflict despite the states of fragility that surround large-scale operations and of which they become part. What also emerges from the analysis, however, is the proposition that a deliberate and more limited focus on conflict management can be an effective strategy for reducing fragility itself.

As illustrated by the examples of Angola and Uganda, contexts are typically fragile at least in part because the dominant political structures contribute to the risk factors for conflict and violence, rather than to their solutions. Yet because these systems are functioning to achieve some purpose – protecting the power and authority of a particular elite, for example – they are highly resistant to change. This is not only a national but also a local phenomenon. The inability or unwillingness of traditional authorities in West Africa to adapt the allocation of communal land to the realities of changing demographics, for example – which would reduce the resources controlled by current landholders – was found to be a significant contributing factor to the large numbers of young men lacking social or professional attachment, and thus their availability for recruitment into the various brutal conflicts of the region.[94]

Successful conflict management initiatives provide compensatory mechanisms within such fragile systems. Tending to operate in socio-political 'grey' spaces that are neither apart from nor fully part of the fragile state structures,[95] they can through informal channels build more inclusive forums as they analyse conflict, interrupt escalation and resolve grievances. The actions of 'the other' become more knowable and more predictable, opening doors to new possibilities for action that cuts across conflict divides. Furthermore, the evidence suggests that the relationship and trust-building achieved through such efforts can prevent further local conflict, even if national fragility persists.[96] Successful conflict management initiatives may additionally be transitional measures. The Independent Mediation Service of South Africa, an institution that emerged from private rather than public negotiations to manage increasingly violent conflict between mining houses and black unions in apartheid South Africa, for example, became the blueprint for the new government's Commission for Conciliation, Mediation and Arbitration (CCMA), which resolves employment grievances. The CCMA is often pointed to as a reasonably effective mechanism within a still-volatile labour environment. It turns out that tackling conflict on its own terms opens spaces for further progress towards reduced fragility.

Notes

1. Based on average violent death rates in the period 2004–2009. See Geneva Declaration Secretariat (GDS), *Global Burden of Armed Violence* (Geneva: GDS, 2011), p. 6.
2. See Randal C. Archibold, 'Gangs' Truce Buys El Salvador a Tenuous Peace', *New York Times*, 27 August 2012.
3. Committee in Solidarity with the People of El Salvador (CiSPES), 'Salvadoran Government Accused of Negotiating with Gangs, After 40% Drop in Murders', 20 April 2012.
4. Chris von der Borgh and Wim Savenije, 'De-securitising and Re-securitising Gang Policies: The Funes Government and Gangs in El Salvador', *Journal of Latin American Studies*, vol. 487, no. 1, 2014, pp. 1, 21.
5. Ana Glenda Táger and Isabel Aguilar Umaña, *La Tregua Entre Pandillas Salvadoreñas Hacia un Proceso de Construcción de Paz Social* (Guatemala City: Interpeace, 2013); Teresa Whitfield, *Mediating Criminal Violence: Lessons from the Gang Truce in El Salvador* (Geneva: Centre for Humanitarian Dialogue, 2013).
6. Isabel Aguilar Umaña, Bernardo Arevalo de León and Ana Glenda Táge, 'El Salvador: Negotiating with Gangs', in Alexander Ramsbotham and Achim Wennmann (eds), *Legitimacy and Peace Processes: From Coercion to Consent* (London: Conciliation Resources, 2014), pp. 97–8.
7. Gabriela Aguinaga, *Learning from Medellín: A Success Story of Holistic Violence Prevention*, 27 January 2015, http://www.saferspaces.org.za/blog/entry/learning-from-medellin-a-success-story-of-holistic-violence-prevention; Organisation for Economic Co-operation and Development (OECD), *Armed Violence Reduction: Enabling Development* (Paris: OECD, 2009), pp. 97–8. Francisco Gutierrez, Maria Pinto, Juan Carlos Arenas, Tania Guzman and Maria Gutierrez, 'The Importance of Political Coalitions in the Successful Reduction of Violence in Colombian Cities', *Urban Studies*, vol. 50, no. 15, 2013, pp. 3134–51.
8. OECD, *Investing in Security: A Global Assessment of Armed Violence and Reductions Initiatives* (Paris: OECD, 2011), pp. 32, 44–9, 54–8.
9. Rim Turkmani, Mary Kaldor, Wisam Elhamwi, Joan Ayo and Nael Hariri, *Hungry for Peace: Positives and Pitfalls of Local Truces and Ceasefires in Syria* (London: London School of Economics, 2014), p. 44.
10. Pat Johnson and Abdirahman Raghe, 'How Somali-led Peace Processes Work', in Mark Bradbury and Sally Healy (eds), *Whose Peace Is It Anyway? Connecting Somali and International Peacemaking* (London: Conciliation Resources, 2010), pp. 46–9.
11. Roberto Valencia and Carlos Martinez, 'Promoter of Talks with El Salvador's Gangs Loses Faith' (Part 2), *InsightCrime*, 25 October 2015, http://www.insightcrime.org/news-analysis/raul-mijango-interview-el-faro-pt-2?utm_source=Master+List&utm_

campaign=979ee3ab7d-
10_30_1510_28_2015&utm_
medium=email&utm_term=0_
e90c5425f9-979ee3ab7d-267153105.

12 Patricia Justino, Tilman Brück,
and Philip Verwimp, 'Micro-Level
Dynamics of Conflict, Violence, and
Development: A New Analytical
Framework', in Patricia Justino,
Tilman Brück, and Philip Verwimp
(eds), *A Micro-Level Perspective on
the Dynamics of Conflict, Violence,
and Development* (Oxford: Oxford
University Press, 2013), p. 5.

13 Patricia Justino, 'Research and
Policy Implications from a
Micro-Level Perspective on the
Dynamics of Conflict, Violence,
and Development', in Justino,
Brück, and Verwimp, *A Micro-
Level Perspective on the Dynamics of
Conflict, Violence, and Development*,
p. 291.

14 Séverine Autesserre, *The Trouble
with the Congo: Local Violence and the
Failure of International Peacebuilding*
(Cambridge: Cambridge University
Press, 2010), pp. xvii, 2.

15 *Ibid.*

16 *Ibid.*, p. 231.

17 United Nations Development
Programme (UNDP), *Conflict Risk
Mapping Analysis* (Juba: UNDP
South Sudan, 2012).

18 Sergio Duailibi, William Ponicki,
Joel Grube, Ilana Pinsky, Ronaldo
Laranjeira, and Martin Raw, 'The
Effect of Restricting Opening Hours
on Alcohol-Related Violence',
American Journal of Public Health,
vol. 97, no. 12, 2007, pp. 2276–80.

19 GDS, 'Violence Reduction and
Peacebuilding: How Crime and
Violence Observatories Can
Contribute', Report of Expert

Workshop, Geneva, 26–28 June 2013,
http://www.genevadeclaration.
org/events/expert-meetings/
observatories-2013/meeting-report/
iii-session-summaries.html.

20 Lindie Botha with Pablo Lumerman,
*Inclusion: Interview with Antonio
Bernales* (The Hague: ACCESS
Facility, 2015).

21 See OECD, *Evaluating Peacebuilding
Activities in Settings of Conflict and
Fragility – Improving Learning for
Results* (Paris: OECD, 2012), p. 79.

22 CDA Collaborative Learning
Projects Reflecting on Peace
Practice, *Participant Training Manual*
(Cambridge, MA: CDA, 2009).

23 Elisabeth Gilgen and Lauren
Tracey, *Contributing Evidence
to Programming: Armed Violence
Monitoring Systems* (Geneva: GDS,
2011).

24 Nicklas Svensson, 'Are We
Disciplined About Asking
Questions?', in Brian Ganson
(ed.), *Management in Complex
Environments: Questions for Leaders*
(Stockholm: International Council
of Swedish Industry, 2013), pp.
135–7.

25 *Ibid.*, pp. 141–4.

26 Fundación Este País, *Observatorios
Ciudadanos: Ejercer la Ciudadanía en
la Práctica* (Mexico: Fundación Este
País, 2008).

27 Natasha Singer, 'Mission Control,
Built for Cities: I.B.M. Takes
"Smarter Cities" Concept to Rio de
Janeiro', *New York Times*, 3 March
2012.

28 See http://www.ibm.com/
smarterplanet/us/en/smarter_cities/
overview.

29 Analysis and quotations from Pablo
Lumerman and Duncan Autrey,

Chichigalpa Association for Life and Nicaragua Sugar Estates Ltd (The Hague: ACCESS, 2013).

30 See Niger Delta Partnership Initiative (NDPI) Foundation, http://ndpifoundation.org.

31 NDPI, *The Niger Delta Partnership Initiative in Review 2010–2013* (Washington, DC: NDPI, 2014).

32 Graeme Simpson, at the conference 'Connecting the Dots: Linking Peacemaking to Peacebuilding to Development', Geneva, 8 June 2010.

33 Katia Papagianni, *National Dialogue Processes in Political Transitions* (Geneva and Brussels: Centre for Humanitarian Dialogue and European Peacebuilding Liaison Office, 2014), p. 1.

34 *Ibid.*, p. 11.

35 Norwegian Nobel Committee, 'The Nobel Peace Prize for 2015: Press Release', Oslo, 10 October 2015, http://www.nobelprize.org/nobel_prizes/peace/laureates/2015/press.html.

36 Katia Papagianni, 'National Conferences in Transitional Periods: The Case of Iraq', *International Peacekeeping*, vol. 13, no. 3, 2006, pp. 325–6.

37 Thania Paffenholz, 'Civil Society in Peace Negotiations: Beyond the Inclusion–Exclusion Dichotomy', *Negotiation Journal*, vol. 30, no. 1, 2014, pp. 69–91.

38 Achim Wennmann and Alexander Ramsbotham, 'Conclusion: From Coercion to Consent', in Ramsbotham and Wennmann, *Legitimacy and Peace Processes*, p. 116.

39 Extractive Industries Review (EIR), *Striking a Better Balance: The World Bank Group and Extractive Industries*

– Volume I (Washington, DC: EIR, 2003), p. 18.

40 Oxfam, 'Moral Hazard? "Mega" Public–Private Partnerships in African Agriculture' (Oxford: Oxfam, 2014).

41 Interview by Brian Ganson.

42 Botha and Lumerman, *Inclusion*.

43 Lindie Botha with Pablo Lumerman, *The Art of Representation: An Interview with Mia Quiaoit-Corpus* (The Hague: ACCESS, 2015).

44 Cécile Renouard, 'Are We Working Well With Others?', in Ganson, *Management in Complex Environments*, pp. 168–170.

45 Kiikpoye K. Aaron and John M. Patrick, 'Corporate Social Responsibility Patterns and Conflicts in Nigeria's Oil-Rich Region', *International Area Studies Review*, vol. 16, no. 4, 2013, pp. 341–56.

46 Interview by Brian Ganson.

47 Helena Puig Larrauri, Rodrigo Davies, Michaela Ledesma, Jennifer Welch, *New Technologies: The Future of Alternative Infrastructures for Peace* (Geneva: Geneva Peacebuilding Platform, 2015), p. 3.

48 The Global Database on Events, Location and Tone (GDELT) is a freely available database that monitors the world's news media in print, broadcast and web formats, in more than 100 languages, with daily updates. See http://www.gdeltproject.org.

49 Puig Larrauri, Davies, Ledesma, Welch, *New Technologies*, p. 3.

50 See http://cureviolence.org/the-interrupters.

51 See Wesley G. Skogan, Susan M. Hartnett, Natalie Bump, and Jill Dubois, 'Evaluation of Ceasefire

Chicago', 19 March 2009, http://www.skogan.org/files/Evaluation_of_CeaseFire-Chicago_Main_Report.03-2009.pdf. Also see http://cureviolence.org/results/scientific-evaluations/.

52 Simon Mason, *Insider Mediators: Exploring Their Key Role in Informal Peace Processes* (Berlin: Berghof Foundation for Peace Support, 2009).

53 Interview by Brian Ganson.

54 Chevron, 'Chevron Increases Support for Niger Delta Partnership Initiative', Press release, 10 June 2014, http://www.chevron.com/chevron/pressreleases/article/06102014_chevronincreasessupportfornigerdeltapartnershipinitiative.news.

55 See http://p4p-nigerdelta.org/about.

56 Merrick Hoben, David Kovick, David Plumb, and Justin Wright, *Corporate and Community Engagement in the Niger Delta: Lessons Learned from Chevron Nigeria Limited's GMOU Process* (Cambridge: Consensus Building Institute, 2012), pp. 9–10.

57 High Level Panel on Infrastructure, see World Bank, *Overcoming Constraints to the Financing of Infrastructure: Success Stories and Lessons Learned* (Washington, DC: World Bank, 2014), p. 3.

58 Lisa J. Laplante and Suzanne A. Spears, 'Out of the Conflict Zone: The Case for Community Consent Processes in the Extractive Sector', *Yale Human Rights and Development Law Journal*, vol. 11, 2008, p. 115.

59 *Ibid.*, p. 69.

60 United Nations, *Guidance for Effective Mediation* (New York: United Nations, 2012); United Nations Department of Political Affairs (UNDPA) and United Nations Environment Programme (UNEP), *Natural Resources and Conflict: A Guidance for Mediation Practitioners* (New York and Nairobi: UNDPA and UNEP, 2015).

61 John Kania and Mark Kramer, 'Collective Impact', *Stanford Social Innovation Review*, Winter 2011, p. 40.

62 National Peace Council, *Strategic Plan 2013–2017 in Accordance with the National Peace Council's Mandate under Act, 2011 (818) including a Plan to Implement the Peace Fund* (Accra: National Peace Council, 2013).

63 Ministry of Interior of Ghana (MoIG), *National Architecture for Peace in Ghana* (Accra: MoIG, 2006).

64 Compliance Advisor Ombudsman (CAO), *Annual Report 2010 and Review FY 2000–10* (Washington, DC: International Finance Corporation, 2010).

65 Gutierrez, Pinto, Arenas, Guzman and Gutierrez, 'The Importance of Political Coalitions in the Successful Reduction of Violence in Colombian Cities', p. 3143.

66 United Nations Office on Drugs and Crime (UNODC) and World Bank, *Crime, Violence, and Development: Trends, Costs, and Policy Options in the Caribbean* (Vienna and Washington, DC: UNODC and World Bank, 2007), p. 124.

67 Pilar Rukavina de Vidovgrad, *What Role of the Private Sector in the Prevention of Election Violence? The Case of Kenya* (Geneva: Geneva Peacebuilding Platform, 2015), p. 5.

68 Mary B. Anderson and Marshall Wallace, *Opting Out of War: Strategies to Prevent Violent Conflict* (Boulder,

CO: Lynner Rienner, 2013), pp. 10–11.

69 Brian Ganson and Nicklas Svensson, *An Evaluation of Conciliation Resources: Decennial Review, 2000–2010* (Stockholm: Swedish International Development Agency, 2010).

70 Trixie Akpedonu, Ben Lumsdaine and Aminata Sow, *Keeping the Peace: Lessons Learned from Preventive Action towards Kenya's 2013 Elections* (Geneva: Geneva Peacebuilding Platform, 2013), pp. 11–12.

71 Hendrik Kotze, *Mediating Economic Interests in the Context of Xenophobia* (The Hague: ACCESS Facility, 2015).

72 Andries Odendaal, *A Crucial Link: Local Peace Committees and National Peacebuilding* (Washington, DC: United States Institute of Peace, 2013); Chetan Kumar and Jos De la Haye, 'Hybrid Peacemaking: Building National "Infrastructures for Peace"', *Global Governance*, vol. 18, no. 1, 2011, p. 13.

73 Andries Odendaal, *An Architecture for Building Peace at the Local Level: A Comparative Study of Local Peace Committees* (New York: UNDP, 2010).

74 Odendaal, *A Crucial Link*, p. 70.

75 Chris Spies, 'South Africa's National Peace Accord', in Catherine Barnes (ed.), *Owning the Process: Public Participation in Peacemaking* (London: Conciliation Resources, 2002), pp. 20–5.

76 See Niger Delta Partnership Initiative Foundation, http://ndpifoundation.org.

77 Volker Boege, Anne Brown, Kevin Clements and Anna Nolan, 'Building Peace and Political

Community in Hybrid Political Orders', *International Peacekeeping*, vol. 15, no. 5, 2009, p. 606.

78 Ganson and Svensson, *An Evaluation of Conciliation Resources*.

79 *Ibid.*

80 Aaron Ausland and Gerard Tonn, *Partnering for Local Development: An Independent Assessment of a Unique Corporate Social Responsibility and Community Relations Strategy* (Johannesburg: Barrick Gold Corporation, 2010).

81 Patricia I. Vasquez, *Oil Sparks in the Amazon: A Look at Local Conflict, Indigenous Populations, and Natural Resources* (Athens: University of Georgia Press, 2013).

82 Anderson and Wallace, *Opting Out of War*, p. 98.

83 Béatrice Pouligny, *State–Society Relations and Intangible Dimensions of State Resilience and State Building: A Bottom-Up Perspective* (Florence: European University Institute, 2010).

84 Conciliation Resources, 'The International Contact Group on Mindanao', http://www.c-r.org/featured-work/international-contact-group-mindanao.

85 Achim Wennmann, *The Political Economy of Peacemaking* (Abingdon: Routledge, 2011), p. 82.

86 Geneva Peacebuilding Platform, *White Paper on Peacebuilding* (Geneva: Geneva Peacebuilding Platform, 2015), p. 8.

87 George Kohlrieser, *Hostage at the Table: How Leaders Can Overcome Conflict, Influence Others, and Raise Performance* (San Francisco, CA: Jossey-Bass, 2006).

88 I. William Zartman, 'Dynamics and Constraints in Negotiations

in Internal Conflict', in I. William Zartman (ed.), *Elusive Peace: Negotiating an End to Civil Wars* (Washington, DC: Brookings Institution, 1995), p. 20.

89 See, for instance, Bradbury and Healy, *Whose Peace is it Anyway?*; Mary B. Anderson, Dayna Brown, and Isabella Jean, *Time to Listen: Hearing People on the Receiving End of International Aid* (Cambridge, MA: CDA Collaborative Learning Projects, 2013); Antonio Donini, Larry Minear, Ian Smillie, Ted van Baarda and Anthony C. Welch, *Mapping the Security Environment: Understanding the Perceptions of Local Communities, Peace Support Organizations and External Aid Agencies* (Medford, MA: Feinstein International Famine Centre, 2005).

90 Brian Ganson and Achim Wennmann, *Confronting Risk, Mobilizing Action: A Framework for Conflict Prevention in the Context of Large-scale Business Investments*

(Berlin: Friedrich Ebert Stiftung, 2012), p. 4.

91 Paul Eavis, *Working Against Violence: Promising Practices in Armed Violence Reduction and Prevention* (Geneva: GDS, 2011), pp. 57–8.

92 Kumar and De la Haye, 'Hybrid Peacemaking', p. 13.

93 David K. Leonard, *Where are 'Pockets' of Effective Agencies Likely in Weak Governance States and Why? A Propositional Inventory* (Brighton: Institute of Development Studies, 2008).

94 Paul Richards and Jean Pierre Chauveau, *Land, Agricultural Change and Conflict in West Africa: Regional issues from Sierra Leone, Liberia and Côte d'Ivoire* (Paris: OECD, 2007).

95 Ganson and Wennmann, *Confronting Risk, Mobilizing Action*.

96 See Tania Hohe, 'Local Governance after Conflict: Community Development in East Timor', *Journal of Peacebuilding and Development*, vol. 1, no. 3, 2004, pp. 45–56. Anderson and Wallace, *Opting Out of War*.

The case for pragmatic solutions

'Because I'm the head of the state oil company, every morning I go to work and look for oil. But because I love my country, every night I go home and pray we don't find it.'[1] The executive's sentiments reflect the reality of his small nation. Although it will soon be counted among the world's middle-income countries, its population is largely impoverished. In an ideal world, the country could make good use of the royalties, tax revenues, jobs, training, infrastructure development and value chain opportunities that oil and gas exploitation might yield to drive human development. But it is also a country that, after ending a military dictatorship, barely maintains the delicate balancing act in national politics required by intense inter-ethnic rivalries, and whose president is implicated in the arms-for-drugs trade. There are tensions between the capital and the outlying provinces over resources and authority, and in the provinces between poor farmers and even more marginalised indigenous populations over land. Missteps over many years by international mining companies – including land grabs, repressive security measures, water pollution and broken promises to invest in communities – provide the basis for smouldering grievances, overt protest and generalised suspicion of the private sector. Meanwhile, highly organised and internationally financed gangs increasingly engage in illegal mining on an industrial scale, leading to skirmishes with the army. This all plays out against the memory of the country's guerrilla insurgency. Pouring oil revenues into this cauldron, the executive reflected, would be more likely to lead to greater chaos than to accelerated development.

The widening gap between policy and reality

While this is the story of one small country, it describes the dynamics of business and conflict in many of the world's fragile states. Yet neither of the dominant international policy responses surveyed in this book seems well-positioned to help mitigate significant conflict risks with anything like the focus or urgency required to make investment in such places a predictably positive force, rather than a destabilising one. One strand of international policy, addressed in Chapter One, is premised on international business as being fundamentally predatory. Its proponents call for binding international rules for companies and accountability for them before Western courtrooms and transnational tribunals. The other strand of international policy, explored in Chapter Two, takes as its starting point the view that international businesses are paragons of good citizenship. Its proponents call for the building of sound state institutions to manage a liberal economy in which the private sector plays a much more prominent role. Whether or not these policy directions make sense on their own terms – as long-term efforts towards greater justice or sound economic policy – they do not seem to be credible responses to business and conflict in countries such as the one described above.

Both international policies depend upon complex chains of coordinated action. This becomes apparent as we examine for each its 'theory of change', or sequence of assumptions that set out how and why a desired change is expected to happen in a particular context.[2] While these descriptions are admittedly caricatures, those who focus on the negative role of business, broadly speaking, adopt a theory of change as follows: (1) international efforts to define the rules of the game will result in (2) enforcement of greater accountability from companies for their international obligations that will in turn result in (3) better corporate behaviour that (4) mitigates the most important conflicts involving business in fragile states. Those who promote a positive view of business adopt a quite different theory of change, namely: (a) international efforts can reform state institutions in ways that (b) let them effectively manage a liberal economy to (c) unleash private-sector potential in ways that (d) mitigate the most important social and economic deprivations underpinning conflict. For both proposed mechanisms of action, each step is difficult to execute on its own; and any effect on business and conflict is dependent on all of the elements – and therefore a wide range of national and international actors – working in a coordinated manner. This seems unlikely in fragile environments, particularly if the goal is to address endemic and growing conflict and violence within a reasonable time horizon.

Even if such complex policy initiatives could be executed, it would remain hard for those who hope to address the destructive conflict that undermines human rights and peaceful development to put too much faith in either international approach. Focused as they are on creating incentives and disincentives for international companies, these approaches appear to have little to say about the broader dynamics of business and conflict in fragile states surveyed in Chapter Three. These encompass socio-political struggles and violence that, for the most part, are neither directly caused, nor controllable, by any company. Examples include criminal extortion and terror threats, patronage networks and the democratic deficit, generalised labour unrest and divided communities – and the often fumbled responses to these by entrenched elites in control of institutions whose reform they often frustrate. And as the gap between international policy responses and this new face of conflict widens, so too does the gap between these policies and the new trends of investment. Drawing their resources and support from the new Asian Infrastructure Investment Bank or the growing investment of Africa's own pension funds in the continent's major projects,[3] for example, fragile state elites can be less interested in, or dependent on, the international policy agenda as they engage with 'alternative investors, aid donors and trade partners' largely beyond the reach of current policy levers,[4] further undermining state-building efforts as explored in Chapter Four. The international system around which both international policy responses to business and conflict are built is shifting under policymakers' feet.

International policy responses also do not seem particularly attractive even to an ethical company. Within such a company, one entire office may be dedicated to assessing and reporting on compliance with international standards under a variety of compulsory and voluntary mechanisms. Another of its offices may be caught up in the variety of international policy forums and national public–private partnership initiatives meant to promote responsible investment in fragile states. None of these activities, however, help a company that finds itself embroiled in fragile-state dynamics and the conflicts these engender. The stakeholders who make the decisions about conflict or coexistence with the company at the level of its local operations – from community groups and traditional authorities to armed gangs – are neither part of international policy setting nor impressed by the reports produced by corporate initiatives. Nor does the growing trend of promoting good practice guidance for companies appear to have any widespread effect on business and conflict. The impact of such guidance seems particularly weak with regard to political issues at the heart of fragility and violence.[5] Even the normally cheerful UN Global Compact, a UN voluntary initiative to promote human rights, labour, environment and anti-corruption principles within companies, finds that 'Despite efforts to enhance the private sector's capacity to make a positive contribution and to mitigate the negative impact of their operations, individual company and industry initiatives to promote conflict-sensitive practices have not been widely embraced and have not yielded a cumulative positive benefit to conflict-affected communities.'[6] So even in the ideal case where a company invests significant resources to comply with international law and emerging norms, stay within the bounds of its host country's legislation, and engage communities according to what it is told are international best practices, it may still find itself confronting operational disruption, destruction of assets, threats to people, or other forms of conflict and violence. And of course, fragile environments are replete with economic actors who are not nearly so ethical or conscientious.

In brief, contemporary international policy responses offer little that will address acute and widespread risks of conflict and violence related to large-scale business operations in fragile states at anything approaching the scale and speed required. If international policy responses remain focused primarily on the long-term goals of state-building, private-sector promotion and human rights enforcement, business and conflict will increasingly manifest as it does in the example that opens this chapter and in the dozens of other fragile contexts surveyed in this book that are at least as complex. Such destructive conflict demonstrably undermines business and social goals alike. It at the same time undermines attempts to implement laudable and necessary reforms.

A new pair of glasses

Hyperopia, or farsightedness, is a defect of the eye that results in an inability to see near objects, even though distant objects can be seen clearly. Policymakers in international organisations and financial institutions promoting the private sector, as well as advocacy organisations trying to restrain it, similarly appear to view in the distance the promised land of sound institutions, an inclusive economy, respect for international human rights and rule of law for now-fragile states. But they seem unable to see the conflict and violence playing out in front of their eyes, or the perverse effects international policy responses may cause when they do not account for the socio-political struggles unfolding around them. International actors might benefit from a new pair of glasses that helps them focus on immediate-term responses that interrupt the downward spiral of negative interactions among governments, citizens and corporations that all too often drive business-related conflict – and even fragility itself.

One lens of the new pair of glasses would help international policymakers to see business not in isolation – whether as villain or hero, depending on the policy perspective – but as only one element of a complex system that is defined, and therefore must be addressed, primarily at the local level. It is increasingly understood that a company does 'not exist in a vacuum but in the wider community in which it operates'.[7] Companies that expand their presence in conflict-prone and fragile environments become actors in local conflict dynamics, whatever their intentions and whatever the externally imposed norms by which they are guided. At the same time, they are only one of the many mitigating or amplifying factors of conflict and fragility. Such understanding builds from systems approaches in development policy.[8] The Organisation for Economic Co-operation and Development (OECD), for instance, has recently issued a report on 'states of fragility'. The report underlines that fragility is not the same across political and social systems, and that different cases will be characterised by 'the diversity of risk and vulnerabilities that generate fragility in so many forms'.[9] These risks and vulnerabilities include, for instance, climate change, population growth and urbanisation, land disputes, rapid political change and other factors as explored in Chapter Three.

This new lens should help international actors to see that their many isolated projects – whether to create jobs, build a particular state institution, open markets or punish errant companies – will surely not induce the social change required for conflict risk mitigation, violence reduction or stabilisation of fragile places. Frustration and perverse impacts will abound. A jobs creation programme may never get off the ground due to claims from competing ethnic groups that they are being unfairly excluded, while an irrigation project meant to increase local farm yields and incomes makes land so valuable that it becomes worth fighting over. Social innovation research increasingly finds that 'No single organization is responsible for any major social problem, nor can any single organization cure it.'[10] Rather, research suggests that effective social change evolves from a holistic approach that builds on the strategic alignment of actors, interests and resources to achieve a common goal. This means that international focus on private-sector actors and discrete initiatives is insufficient; a systems approach is required.

The other lens of the new pair of glasses would help international actors to move away from an obsessive focus on rules and structures towards adaptive systems of sufficient consensus in fragile states. Such thinking stands in contrast to current policies that focus mainly on the regulatory frameworks and enforcement mechanisms of national governments and international regimes as levers for change. Effective policy on business and conflict in fragile states requires more than reform of international companies or national governments as implicit in decades of fragile-states policy. Rather, it must be an ever-widening conversation with the full range of stakeholders who are implicated in the local conflict dynamics surrounding particular large-scale investments. Through this lens, international actors can recognise that most contemporary state-building approaches hand over the keys to control over business investment and its benefits to the national elite that happens to be in power. Since exclusive and authoritarian regimes are a key driver of fragility and violence, this is highly problematic.

This new lens should also help actors to recognise the troubling 'absence of the local level in fragile states debates'.[11] Many fragile state governments embrace state-building when it means strengthening government capabilities to control the economy, but become opposed to it when it means strengthening state–society relations or expanding opportunities for political representation, justice or welfare as understood by the people most directly impacted by large-scale investment projects. It is particularly at the level of an investment's impact on local states of fragility, the people and interests within them, and their relationships with each other, that international policy and practice might most usefully focus.

Investments in conflict management that work

With new glasses, policymakers may better be able to perceive areas of business investment that are conflict-prone or fragile as fundamentally local, complex systems. A confluence of social, political and economic factors impact the perceptions, attitudes, interests and choices of a variety of actors towards conflict or stability. It should therefore become clear that fragile places are not amenable to 'trickle-down' theories of social change. A persistent attitude prevails in many policy circles that peaceful development can evolve from macro-level changes that then somehow manifest at the micro level: for example, the still-prevalent mental model that opening trade leads to growth, growth to prosperity, and prosperity to peace, without any particular regard to the context in which the model is applied or accounting for the counter-examples that abound.[12]

It is also widely assumed that norms articulated by the UN in Geneva or the World Bank in Washington can be 'nationalised' through model legislation or via 'push' projects meant to help fragile states emulate more stable countries, and can thereby change the behaviour of local actors in ways that mitigate risks of conflict and violence. So it is posited by the UN Working Group on the issue of human rights and transnational corporations and other business enterprises, for example, that the Guiding Principles on Business and Human Rights will, through national action plans implemented by fragile-state governments, achieve meaningful changes for people affected by abusive businesses.[13] It appears that this is to be done without asking why those governments have not already taken action, or how this initiative will differ from the host of other policies publicly supported by governments to please donor states but never implemented. Many such efforts towards norm setting, institution building and rule of law may be well intentioned, have some importance for the long term, and be taken seriously by corporate, diplomatic and donor representatives. Yet they have not demonstrated impact at the local level with regard to conflict risk mitigation.

Attempts to address business and conflict in fragile states will falter as long as international actors single out the actions of the private sector or the national government in isolation from other stakeholders; confound efforts to build the capacities of the government in power with authentic state-building, which arises from the emergence of sufficient social consensus; rely on new laws or regulatory regimes as strong levers for change; or more generally believe that externally directed interventions can provide a lasting solution to conflict and security problems in fragile states. These observations may sound familiar to readers with experience outside business and finance; they reflect the broad contours of good practice in the development and peacebuilding spheres. The mantras of 'local first' and 'bottom-up' have emerged over at least three decades of hard-won experience. The *New Deal for Engagement in Fragile States*,[14] the World Bank *World Development Report 2011: Conflict, Security and Development*,[15] and most contemporary donor guidance emphasise local leadership and ownership (not to be confused with national government ownership), as well as inclusive political settlements and conflict resolution. Field research and countless personal testimonies demonstrate how international actors consistently overestimate their capacities to bring peace and development to conflict-prone and fragile environments. They also emphasise how disconnected international efforts may be from local contexts. Despite their failure so far to be integrated into international policy and practice on business and conflict in fragile states, these conclusions fall well within contemporary mainstream policy discourse in development and peacebuilding.

It should therefore not be surprising that the most promising approaches to business and conflict in fragile states comprise archetypical peacebuilding and conflict management practices adapted to local conflicts of which companies become part. As surveyed in Chapter Five, these can in general terms be described as a set of interconnected building blocks:

institutionalised mechanisms or networks for monitoring the local context; the rallying of diverse and sometimes conflicting local stakeholders around high-quality data and trustworthy analysis; dialogue that builds sufficient consensus for action; proactive conflict prevention and resolution interventions; and a backbone support organisation that facilitates expert and neutral assistance. Such approaches promote the prioritisation of conflict prevention or violence reduction efforts by coalitions that cut across social and political divides, as well as the coordination of efforts across a variety of sectors and actors. They succeed in fragile states despite social divisions, weak institutions, a lack of trust in government, legacies of grievance from the past, pressing socio-economic challenges or the presence of spoilers – conditions that prove to undermine efforts through the dominant policy responses of private-sector promotion and human rights enforcement. They manage fragility by engaging parties on the basis of their partisan interests and desires to mitigate their own risks; creating vertical linkages from local conflicts to influential actors at regional, national or international levels; building from existing social and political capital and functioning institutions whether formal or informal; and providing outside intervention in the more acceptable forms of expertise and advice. From the company–community *mesas de diálogo* ('dialogue tables') that are increasingly common in Latin America to the peace committees sponsored by Chevron in Nigeria, such approaches work to manage business and conflict, even in fragile contexts.

International accompaniment for local conflict management

More conflict will be avoided and fewer existing conflicts exacerbated as international actors change their unit of analysis from the national level to the local contexts in which individual large-scale businesses operate. The degree to which the World Bank's new mantra of 'security, justice and jobs'[16] proves a sound formulation for addressing fragility remains to be tested. But the analysis of this book should make clear that its primary focus on national-level perspectives and projects – which typically produce some jobs over here, and a bit of justice sector or security sector reform over there, unrelated to specific local dynamics of conflict and violence – is unlikely to meaningfully contribute to reductions in conflict or fragility. Rather, progress comes through holistic approaches, which the evidence demonstrates are more workable at the local than at the national level.

Local strategies to manage conflict in the context of large-scale business investments succeed where national-level state-building, private-sector promotion and rule-of-law initiatives fail because the local approach is more targeted to local conditions, faster and better adapted to fragile environments. The operative theory of change is that (1) the local actors most invested in a problem (2) who are convened to work together on the basis of their own self-interest (3) can combine an improved understanding of local dynamics with strategic outside advice (4) to plan solutions for which there is sufficient consensus for action. Effective strategies tackle manifestations of conflict – whether company versus community, labour versus management, or extortionist gang versus local business – at a local level, while linking to supportive actors at other levels. They compensate for the lack of legitimate state institutions with more inclusive, built-for-purpose mechanisms that analyse conflict, interrupt its escalation, resolve grievances and put in place locally credible plans to address root causes. They are, in the parlance of development, locally rooted.

There are, however, vital roles to be played by donors and development agencies, international firms and financial institutions, companies and international labour organisations, foundations and advocacy groups.

The first role for international actors in addressing business-related conflict in fragile states might best be described in terms of restraint. It builds from 'conflict sensitivity' practice that is grounded in the imperative 'of systematically taking into account both the positive and negative impact of interventions, in terms of conflict or peace dynamics, on contexts in which they are undertaken, and, conversely, the impact of these on the interventions'.[17] A seminal study focusing on the involvement of international donors in developing countries concludes that 'when international assistance is given in the context of a violent conflict, it becomes a part of that context and thus also of the conflict'.[18] This applies also to the policy and institutional reforms that many international actors promote: these can either exacerbate or ameliorate conflict, depending on how they interact with the specific local context in which they are pushed forward. It is insufficient to argue that a policy intervention is good in the abstract, for example, lowering barriers to trade or increasing foreign direct investment (FDI). If, as in Nigeria, rapidly implemented free trade destroys a leading industry to the extent that unemployed youth in certain regions can more easily be recruited to extremist violence, the balance sheet of the intervention goes quickly into the red, whatever the economics textbooks may say. Similarly, if substantially increased FDI in agriculture results in tensions between agribusiness and local communities escalating faster than local institutions can manage, then the resulting conflict and violence will erase any benefits of the promised jobs or technology transfers. International actors could do much good simply by applying conflict sensitivity analyses to their own policy interventions – and by holding each other to account for doing so.

The related principle of 'do no harm' holds that, if outside intervention is to be constructive, 'assistance given in conflict settings ... be provided so that, rather than exacerbating and worsening the conflict, it helps local people disengage from fighting and develop systems for settling the problems which prompt conflict within their societies'.[19] In other words, we can assume that no international project can have a net positive effect on conflict and violence if it drives people apart rather than bringing them together. International actors who succumb to the urge to arrive with substantive policy answers for economic and policy development will be less effective than those who rally diverse local actors to build context-specific understanding of problems as an entry point for change.

Adopting such a mindset would represent a fundamental departure from the prevailing adherence to blueprint policy designs – such as the ones described in Chapters Three and Four – that are often mainly achieved in collaboration with national economic and political elites, and therefore often prove divisive among local stakeholders. Approaches such as problem-driven iterative adaptation (PDIA), by contrast, invest in 'processes of finding and fitting locally relevant solutions to locally felt problems' by 'building broad groups of agents to diagnose, define, implement, and diffuse change ideas'.[20] They recognise that, in the fragile state context, outside reform ideas often have little chance of being fully embraced or implemented. Outside interveners therefore more usefully 'focus on creating an enabling environment for stability and inclusivity',[21] rather than on attempting to provide remedies for the grievances or deprivations that are associated with a particular fragile environment per se. This shifts international attention and resources towards the more manageable and actionable activities of helping local actors to understand and decide how to address in their local context a key driver of fragility: their difficulty in forging a sufficiently broad and influential coalition to address their society's most pressing economic and social challenges.

International actors could start to put conflict sensitivity and do-no-harm principles into action by supporting better local data collection and local facilitation of collaborative analysis as a public good. Chapter Five highlighted that pragmatic solutions can emerge when action is based on detailed information, insight and analysis of local conflict and power dynamics. But it is exactly this type of knowledge that is frequently missing in rumour-rich and information-poor fragile contexts. This is a challenge for businesses, governments, international actors and local communities alike. Each actor may compensate by commissioning its own context and conflict analyses, but these can be duplicative, limited in scope, one-off efforts tied to specific projects or funding cycles and – particularly if carried out by international consultants – expensive. Additionally, optimal risk reduction and conflict mitigation strategies emerging from the analysis will often require coordination with other actors. One factory cannot on its own, for example, address labour protest and violence arising from conflicts in the industry as a whole. Even high-quality analysis is therefore not actionable by the commissioning organisation, and may do little to help prevent or manage business-related conflict and violence.

These challenges are addressed as international actors support local honest brokers who act as conflict observatories for particular geographies or business sectors, facilitating participatory data collection methods and convening diverse parties for collaborative analysis. These observatories could produce higher-quality data, updated continuously and likely to be achieved at a lower cost. They could support a shift over time towards evidence-based planning and action. In the context of business and conflict, their role in harmonising understanding may be particularly important to achieve mobilisation and coordination across peacebuilding, development, government, human rights and private-sector actors with their different languages, world views, time frames, and analytic approaches towards fragile contexts. Such observatories could also be put in place as new sectors are targeted for development in fragile states, informing both policy and investment decisions before commercial operations start.

Institutionalisation of the observatory function is required, both to sustain the conversation around better data and to provide a trusted intermediary between often-conflicting parties. Indeed, 'the expectation that collaboration can occur without a supporting infrastructure is one of the most frequent reasons why it fails'.[22] Yet backbone support organisations for data collection, analysis, joint reflection and coordination of planning are typically difficult to finance because they produce few measurable outputs for funders, because they mainly work discretely and because visible successes are owned by participating members. International actors must therefore confront their own 'reluctance to pay for infrastructure and preference for short-term solutions'.[23]

Another important role for international actors and institutions could be support for local conflict prevention and resolution efforts tied to particular large-scale investments. International financial and development institutions currently may require social impact assessments before major projects are launched or expanded, even demanding elaborate risk mitigation plans. They may set up international grievance mechanisms to hear, often years after the fact, that communities were all the same wrongfully displaced by a palm oil plantation, that a factory engaged in intimidation or murder to suppress labour issues, or that fear over environmental practices resulted in roadblocks or burning tyres that blocked access to a mine. In between, they do little at the local level even with regard to high-risk projects, allowing conflict and fragility to compound.

Building on local capabilities for better data and analysis, international actors could mandate and support at least within their own sphere of influence proactive, locally fair and legitimate, third-party systems for rights protection and dispute resolution – in its simplest terms, referees on the ground where business and conflict can be expected to unfold – before crises occur. In this way, jobs or other benefits of private-sector investment, justice for workers and communities who feel aggrieved by a business operation or its impacts, and security achieved through proactive conflict risk mitigation efforts all come together at the same time and place. A focus on fostering local justice within larger fragile systems is swifter and surer than premising the benefits of business or the reduction of conflict on the reform of all of a fragile state government at once. Furthermore, these islands of effectiveness can serve as examples and anchors for broader social change. They can both compensate for fragile local systems and help transition towards ones that are less so.

A call for business leadership

Neither company shareholders nor development advocates need to, or should, accept the current disconnect between international policy towards business and conflict in fragile states, and tested, mainstream practice to prevent conflict and mitigate risks. While action is required across a variety of sectors, there is a special call to action for international business, for its own and the greater good. As in Anglo American's efforts to achieve a workable relationship with its black unions under the apartheid regime (described in Chapter Two), resulting in the establishment of the Independent Mediation Service of South Africa (IMSSA) and its successes in reducing conflict and violence, private efforts have perhaps a better chance of breaking the institutional reform deadlock in conflict-prone and otherwise fragile places than those pursued by international institutions or national authorities.

Business examples that echo the broad evidence base from armed violence reduction, conflict management and peacebuilding practice, outlined in Chapter Five, should provide confidence that practical, implementable approaches are available to companies, and that these approaches have a far greater chance of achieving positive outcomes for business and society within a faster time frame than current international policy approaches.

For companies to move forward on their implementation, however, their leaders must admit that business is part and parcel of the fragile context, including its complex socio-political dynamics. Particularly for the large-footprint investments with which this book is primarily concerned, business is a significant factor in mitigating or escalating conflict and fragility well beyond the boundaries of its own operations. These dynamics make investments and operations part of a political economy, and inherently political. This remains difficult to accept for many actors, whether in UN headquarters, World Bank offices, civil society forums or corporate boardrooms. As one global executive put it, 'Weren't they telling me just a few decades ago to get *out* of politics?'.[24] Yet to make sense of and address the dynamics of business-related conflict in fragile states, corporate leaders must both admit, and claim the legitimacy to assert, business interests in 'political' matters of conflict, justice and peace.

Many corporations have taken small steps in this direction. At least at the level of corporate policy, most global companies acknowledge that it is in their best interest to manage their own operations in ways that help to strengthen dispute resolution and governance institutions. This is reflected in an ever-growing number of voluntary and multi-stakeholder initiatives. There are also signs that at least some company leaders recognise that they are stakeholders in broader efforts to promote long-term socio-political stability, and that this requires the capacity to work locally with both public officials and the communities impacted by their operations. In this sense, there is a nascent understanding of 'business in society' rather than 'business and society'. Yet most companies appear hesitant to commit the necessary social, political or technical resources required to achieve conflict risk mitigation and violence reduction in and around the communities in which they operate.

This analysis leads to a crossroads for business leaders. Failing to respond to business-related conflict – let alone exploiting fragile-state dynamics – will lead to further division and conflict within already stressed communities and countries. Yet it will admittedly be challenging to implement the collaborative approaches to conflict management outlined in this book. Business in fragile states operates where legacies of the past – whether colonialism, disrespect for human rights, apartheid or other – cast long shadows, and where community mistrust is rampant (and if business is honest in its review of history, often enough justified). 'It's a long journey,' said Lonmin's CEO Ben Magara, brought in after the Marikana massacre in South Africa, 'to win trust from stakeholders and create shared value and purpose.'[25] So the business leader who is deciding whether or not to use the company's weight of influence and resources to tip the balance in favour of local conflict prevention and violence reduction efforts must contemplate a new and substantial level of commitment.

This is not so different, however, from other crossroads faced by business leaders. Until relatively recently, for example, worker deaths and injuries were seen as unfortunate but inevitable occurrences. Yet industry has now become remarkably sophisticated in its understanding of holistic approaches to workplace and, increasingly, community safety, linking these to a company's long-term sustainability and even its identity. Here, the story of Paul O'Neill may be instructive. Giving his first speech as CEO of a faltering Alcoa in 1987, he talked only about worker safety, refusing questions on those issues cared most about by investors, such as the failed products that had led to rising inventories. Wall Street analysts initially turned against him. Yet over his tenure, Alcoa's worker days lost to injury dropped by approximately 90%, while profits roughly quintupled.[26] O'Neill had the vision to see how a higher purpose could fundamentally improve the long-term opportunities available to the company, and the character to demand accountability for safety dynamics and outcomes outside company managers' direct control.

This book has surveyed analogous business successes in fragile environments as companies integrate conflict prevention and violence reduction into their business strategies and operations, and their leaders take accountability for improving conflict dynamics they can influence but not control: a company that avoided the rebel attacks plaguing its competitors by cultivating strong relations with its formerly combative union; another that not only survived, but thrived during a revolution in the Middle East by linking its success to that of its smallholder farmer suppliers as an explicit strategy for conflict risk mitigation; Chevron's attentiveness to community capacities for conflict prevention and resolution in the Niger Delta; and many more. To accelerate progress in the arena of business and conflict in fragile states, O'Neill's degree of business leader clarity, purpose and long-term commitment will need to be applied to conflict management – between the company and local actors, but also between local actors themselves – as a foundation for business success.

Business leaders can take comfort in the recognition that they already have meaningful experience managing conflict in fragile contexts. Companies help ensure collaborative relationships with their most important business partners in difficult places through, for example, a foundational agreement on the purpose of their joint undertaking, legal commitments to specific obligations and expectations, a joint management structure for proactive monitoring of key performance metrics, and graduated dispute resolution clauses in contracts that anticipate the need for facilitated negotiations or mediation. Similarly, businesses ensure access to justice for themselves in fragile environments through independent arbitration clauses with governments under investment treaties, or binding, third-party mechanisms for resolving disputes with other businesses. In these practices companies can find seeds, for example, for the observatory function, dialogue that builds sufficient consensus for action, and proactive conflict interruption. The question for business leaders becomes how to apply analogous principles and practices to help implement a new social contract with community members and other local stakeholders through commitment to, and support for, effective conflict risk assessment, conflict risk mitigation and conflict management strategies.[27]

Pragmatic coalitions for change

This book points to the numerous cases in which insufficient attention to conflict dynamics has led to colossal project failures, for example, multibillion-dollar investments made in mines now idled by community protest, or, in the Uganda example that opens the book, oil companies required to reassess their presence within the country in light of the broader socio-political dynamics, despite hundreds of millions of dollars invested. And in many more places for many more companies, business expansion and revenue growth predicted in optimistic strategic plans are quietly downplayed as the realities of conflict on the ground unfold. These and many other examples lead to assertions, for example by the OECD, that 'MNEs [multinational enterprises] have a strong business incentive to act responsibly'.[28]

Yet, based on a measured review of the evidence, this book is cautious about broad claims to a 'business case' that compels companies towards better management of conflict. Global businesses and financial institutions evaluate risk and returns on a portfolio rather than a project basis, meaning that a failure in one fragile state may be offset by a dozen other profitable ventures. As one high-level executive asserted, 'Your anecdotes of failure don't explain our group performance.'[29] Markets are voting with their feet for more fragile state investment; aggregate financial returns in even difficult places appear remarkably strong, despite conflict risks.

At the same time, the extraordinary difficulty with which international institutions change their world views or strategies suggests that international policy will not change company calculus towards conflict and violence any time soon; it will, rather, continue its increasingly peripheral attempts to manage business and conflict through the creation of incentives and disincentives for business – despite the shifting composition of MNEs and international finance, the consolidation of control over the levers of the economy by fragile state governments, the new strategic landscape of violence and the enduring profitability of less scrupulous enterprises in fragile places. Due to these systemic and institutional constraints, global companies may find it politically and commercially viable to accept conflict as a cost of doing business for some time to come.

This book rather makes a more pragmatic claim: determined efforts to reduce conflict and violence can work, even in the most fragile contexts. The evidence indicates that parties, motivated by their own self-interest, will collaborate on conflict risk mitigation and violence reduction efforts despite starkly different priorities and perspectives. It also shows that efforts can be instigated by a range of forward-looking actors, including businesses, community advocates, international financial institutions, aid agencies, a host country government or any other actor seeking to reduce business-related conflict in a fragile context. Furthermore, there are networks, resources and expertise that can bridge the gaps among these disparate actors. The creation of a coalition against conflict and violence still requires courageous leadership. Those who step forward should be reassured, however, that effective approaches are readily available to help manage business-related conflict in fragile states. These solutions can help manage today's conflicts today, while helping to clear a path for business to be a foundation for peaceful development tomorrow.

Notes

1   Interview by Brian Ganson.
2   Isabel Vogel, Review of the Use of 'Theory of Change' in International Development, Review Report commissioned by the UK Department of International Development (DFID), April 2012, http://r4d.dfid.gov.uk/pdf/outputs/mis_spc/DFID_ToC_Review_VogelV7.pdf.
3   See Patrick McGroarty, 'African Pensions Funds Invest in Infrastructure Projects', Wall Street Journal, 7 May 2015.
4   Will Jones and Ricardo Soares de Oliveira, Africa's Illiberal State-Builders (Oxford: Refugees Studies Centre, 2013), p. 19.

5   Tessa Hebb, Heather Hachigian and Rupert Allen, 'Measuring the Impact of Engagement in Canada', in Tessa Hebb (ed.), The Next Generation of Responsible Investing (Dordrecht: Springer, 2012).
6   United Nations Global Compact (UNGC) and Principles for Responsible Investment, Guidance on Responsible Business in Conflict-Affected and High-Risk Areas: A Resource for Companies and Investors (New York: UNGC, 2010), p. 7.
7   Marilise Smurthwaite, 'The Purpose of the Corporation', in Oliver F. Williams (ed.), Peace Through Commerce (Notre Dame, IN:

University of Notre Dame Press, 2008), p. 19.

8   Cedric de Coning, 'Understanding Peacebuilding as Essentially Local', *Stability*, vol. 2, no. 1, 2013, pp. 1–6; Organisation for Economic Co-operation and Development (OECD), *Applications of Complexity Science for Public Policy: New Tools for Finding Unanticipated Consequences and Unrealized Opportunities* (Paris: OECD, 2009); Mary B. Anderson and Peter Woodrow, *Rising from the Ashes: Development Strategies in Times of Disaster* (Boulder, CO: Lynne Rienner, 1998).

9   OECD, *States of Fragility: Meeting Post-2015 Ambitions* (OECD: Paris, 2015), p. 9.

10 John Kania and Mark Kramer, 'Collective Impact', *Stanford Social Innovation Review*, Winter 2011, pp. 38–9.

11 Marjoke Oosterom, *Fragility at the Local Level: Challenges to Building Local State–Citizen Relations in Fragile Settings* (The Hague and Utrecht: Hivos and ICCO, 2009).

12 See Peter Middlebrook, *Building a 'Fragile Consensus': Liberalisation and State Fragility* (Paris: OECD, 2012).

13 UN Working Group on Business and Human Rights (UNWGBHR), *Guidance on National Action Plans on Business and Human Rights* (Geneva: UNWGBHR, 2015).

14 OECD, *A New Deal for Engagement in Fragile States* (Paris: OECD, 2011).

15 World Bank, *World Development Report 2011: Conflict, Security and Development* (Washington, DC: World Bank, 2011).

16 *Ibid.*, p. 2.

17 Africa Peace Forum, Centre for Conflict Resolution, Consortium of Humanitarian Agencies, Forum on Early Warning and Early Response, International Alert, and Saferworld, 'Introduction', in *Conflict-Sensitive Approaches to Development, Humanitarian Assistance and Peacebuilding: A Resource Pack* (2004), http://www.international-alert.org/sites/default/files/Training_DevelopmentHumanitarianAssistancePeacebuilding_EN_2004_0.pdf.

18 Mary B. Anderson, *Do No Harm: How Aid Can Support Peace – or War* (Boulder, CO: Lynner Rienner, 1999), p. 1.

19 CDA Collaborative Learning Projects, *Reflecting on Peace Practice Project* (Cambridge, MA: CDA Collaborative Learning Projects, 2004).

20 Matt Andrews, *The Limits of Institutional Reform in Development: Changing Rules for Realistic Solutions* (Cambridge: Cambridge University Press, 2014), p. 217.

21 Middlebrook, *Building a 'Fragile Consensus'*, p. 35.

22 Kania and Kramer, 'Collective Impact', p. 40.

23 *Ibid.*, p. 41.

24 Interview by Brian Ganson.

25 Mervin Meintjies, 'Marikana Hangs over Lonmin AGM', *Business Day Live*, 30 January 2015.

26 Charles Duhigg, *The Power of Habit* (London: Random House, 2012).

27 Brian Ganson and Hendrik Kotze, *The Community Contract: Applying Proven Solutions to Familiar Problems* (Cape Town: Africa Centre for Dispute Settlement, 2015).

28 OECD, *Guidelines for Multinational Enterprises: Responsible Business Conduct Matters* (Paris: OECD, 2014), p. 3.

29 Interview by Brian Ganson.

INDEX

Adelphi books are published eight times a year by Routledge Journals, an imprint of Taylor & Francis, 4 Park Square, Milton Park, Abingdon, Oxfordshire OX14 4RN, UK.

A subscription to the institution print edition, ISSN 1944-5571, includes free access for any number of concurrent users across a local area network to the online edition, ISSN 1944-558X. Taylor & Francis has a flexible approach to subscriptions enabling us to match individual libraries' requirements. This journal is available via a traditional institutional subscription (either print with free online access, or online-only at a discount) or as part of our libraries, subject collections or archives. For more information on our sales packages please visit www.tandfonline.com/librarians_pricinginfo_journals.

2016 Annual Adelphi Subscription Rates			
Institution	£651	$1,144 USD	€965
Individual	£230	$393 USD	€314
Online only	£570	$1,001 USD	€844

Dollar rates apply to subscribers outside Europe. Euro rates apply to all subscribers in Europe except the UK and the Republic of Ireland where the pound sterling price applies. All subscriptions are payable in advance and all rates include postage. Journals are sent by air to the USA, Canada, Mexico, India, Japan and Australasia. Subscriptions are entered on an annual basis, i.e. January to December. Payment may be made by sterling cheque, dollar cheque, international money order, National Giro, or credit card (Amex, Visa, Mastercard).

For a complete and up-to-date guide to Taylor & Francis journals and books publishing programmes, and details of advertising in our journals, visit our website: **http://www.tandfonline.com.**

Ordering information:

USA/Canada: Taylor & Francis Inc., Journals Department, 530 Walnut Street, Suite 850, Philadelphia, PA 19106, USA. **UK/Europe/Rest of World:** Routledge Journals, T&F Customer Services, T&F Informa UK Ltd., Sheepen Place, Colchester, Essex, CO3 3LP, UK.

Advertising enquiries to:

USA/Canada: The Advertising Manager, Taylor & Francis Inc., 530 Walnut Street, Suite 850, Philadelphia, PA 19106, USA. Tel: +1 (800) 354 1420. Fax: +1 (215) 207 0050. **UK/Europe/Rest of World**: The Advertising Manager, Routledge Journals, Taylor & Francis, 4 Park Square, Milton Park, Abingdon, Oxfordshire OX14 4RN, UK. Tel: +44 (0) 20 7017 6000. Fax: +44 (0) 20 7017 6336.

The print edition of this journal is printed on ANSI conforming acid-free paper by Bell & Bain, Glasgow, UK.